ETHIOPIA

in Pictures

Jeffrey Zuehlke

Lerner Publications Company

Contents

Lerner Publications Company
A division of Lerner Publishing Group
241 First Avenue North
Minneapolis, MN 55401 U.S.A.

Website address: www.lernerbooks.com

web enhanced @ www.vgsbooks.com

Library of Congress Cataloging-in-Publication Data

Zuehlke, Jeffrey, 1968–
    Ethiopia in pictures / by Jeffrey Zuehlke.
        p. cm. — (Visual geography series)—Rev. and expanded.
    Summary: A historical and current look at Ethiopia, discussing the land, the government, the culture, the people, and the economy.
    Includes bibliographical references and index.
    ISBN: 0-8225-1170-3 (lib. bdg. : alk. paper)
    1. Ethiopia—Pictorial works—Juvenile literature. [1. Ethiopia.] I. Title. II. Visual geography series [Minneapolis, Minn.]
DT374.3.Z84 2005
963—dc22   2003019640

Manufactured in the United States of America
1 2 3 4 5 6 - BP - 10 09 08 07 06 05

INTRODUCTION

For many people, mention of the country Ethiopia will immediately bring up heartbreaking images of starving children living in desolate refugee camps. And indeed, recurring and devastating famine remains the country's greatest challenge in the 2000s, as it has been since the 1970s. But such images are only one picture of the broader mosaic of this large and diverse country, home to some eighty different ethnic groups.

Ethiopia is one of Africa's oldest nations, with a history of rulers dating back more than three thousand years. And while European powers invaded, occupied, and colonized the rest of the continent in the past few centuries, a succession of strong rulers helped Ethiopia resist this fate. The country has remained an independent nation for nearly all of its history.

Between three thousand and four thousand years ago, Sabaean travelers from Sheba, a country on the southern part of the Arabian Peninsula, crossed the Red Sea and began to settle along the east coast

of Africa. They mingled with the many native groups of the area, producing over time a mixed race of farmers, herders, and traders. The earliest known ruler of this period is Maqueda, the queen of Sheba, who is mentioned in the Bible and who is believed to have lived in the tenth century B.C. With a few exceptions and interruptions, Ethiopian rulers claimed descent from the queen of Sheba's line until the 1970s. During that time, the country became a seat for early Christianity in Africa, endured numerous civil wars, and resisted invasions—first from Muslims, beginning in the seventh century, and then from Europeans in the nineteenth century.

Italy conquered Ethiopia in 1936 and occupied the country for five years before Ethiopian and British forces drove out the Italians during World War II (1939–1945). In the postwar years, the policies of Emperor Haile Selassie, who had come to power in 1930, became increasingly unpopular. Then, in 1974, a group of military officers deposed him, replacing the centuries-old monarchy with a socialist government led

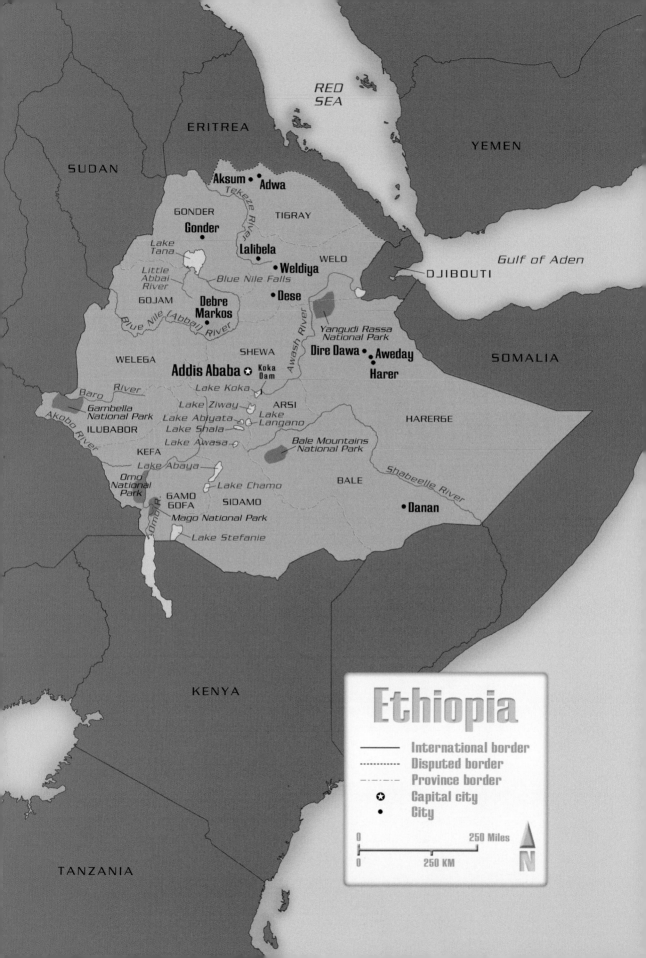

by dictator Mengistu Haile-Mariam. The Mengistu regime's socialist policies promised a better life for ordinary Ethiopians, but the new ideas were largely unsuccessful, and the nation struggled to develop economically. Most Ethiopians remained poor, and a lack of good roads and irrigation systems left many vulnerable to devastating famines, one of which struck in the mid-1980s, affecting millions.

Meanwhile, Mengistu's harsh rule, which included the imprisonment and execution of political opponents, was threatened by forces both internal and external. Ethiopia's neighbor Somalia sought to expand its territory by invading Ethiopia's southeastern regions, while antigovernment forces waged war against Mengistu's regime. In 1991, facing defeat at the hands of the antigovernment forces, Mengistu fled Ethiopia.

A new democratic government was formed, led by Meles Zenawi. Ethiopia enjoyed successful harvests and gradual economic progress in the early 1990s. In 1993 the northern province of Eritrea voted overwhelmingly for self-rule. The leaders of the Eritrean independence movement hoped to bring an end to decades of internal conflict between Ethiopia and its former province. But in 1998, disputes over the two countries' border erupted into a costly war that lasted more than two years. The conflict ended in 2000, but the border issue is still unresolved. Meanwhile, four consecutive years of drought created another humanitarian crisis, with about 14 million Ethiopians requiring international food aid for survival. In 2003 the drought finally ended and the country enjoyed its best harvest in five years. Still, Ethiopia's rapidly growing population continues to stretch the country's resources, and famine continues to affect millions of the nation's citizens.

THE LAND

Ethiopia lies in northeastern Africa in a region known as the Horn of Africa. Occupying an area of 426,373 square miles (1,104,301 square kilometers), Ethiopia is larger than the states of Texas and New Mexico combined. Roughly triangular in shape, it is bordered by Sudan in the west, Kenya in the south, Somalia in the east, Djibouti in the northeast, and Eritrea in the north.

Boundaries

Ethiopia's border with Sudan, one of the longest boundaries on the African continent, was created in 1902. This international boundary cuts through the mountainous western highlands of Ethiopia. In the southwest, the border is defined by the Akobo River, which eventually joins the White Nile River in southern Sudan.

The nation's boundary with Djibouti came into being in 1935 as a result of a territorial agreement between France and Italy, who ruled the two African countries at the time. Ethiopia's southern border with

Kenya was established in the 1950s in cooperation with Great Britain, Kenya's colonial power until its independence in 1963.

Similarly, the border between Ethiopia and Somalia was defined by agreements established between 1897 and 1908 among Italy, Great Britain, and Ethiopia. The United Nations (UN) redefined the boundary in 1950. In the past three decades, Ethiopia has experienced several disputes with Somalia over their mutual boundary. Somalia's belief in the concept of a greater Somalia—one nation for all people of Somali heritage who live on the Horn of Africa (including areas of eastern Ethiopia)—has been one of the motives behind a long series of border conflicts.

Ethiopia has been a landlocked country since 1993, when the province of Eritrea gained its formal independence and took possession of its ports on the Red Sea. This has forced Ethiopia to rely solely on the port of the city of Djibouti for the import and export of goods.

The exact border between Ethiopia and Eritrea has been in dispute since 1993. In May 1998, Ethiopia and Eritrea went to war over the border placement issue. After more than two years of bitter fighting, the two countries signed a peace agreement in June 2000. But despite the efforts of United Nations negotiators and the presence of UN peacekeeping troops in the disputed region, Eritrea and Ethiopia have yet to agree on a defined border. The threat of another war breaking out between the two countries remains.

Topography

Two landforms—the Central Plateau and the Great Rift Valley—dominate Ethiopia's topography, covering more than half of the country's landmass. The rest of the country is made up of the Lowlands, which are scattered along the country's borderlands.

THE CENTRAL PLATEAU Although Ethiopia's central feature is a plateau, it is, in fact, a rugged piece of territory interrupted by small, fertile tablelands (broad, level, and elevated areas), which are often used for growing grain and grazing cattle. The western section of the Central Plateau, sometimes called the Ethiopian Plateau, has heights of 10,000 to 15,000 feet (3,048 to 4,572 meters). The Simyen Mountains rise in this area and include Ras Dashen (15,158 feet/4,620 m), the nation's highest peak. The Ethiopian Plateau receives adequate rain for farming without irrigation and, therefore, has greater agricultural potential than the rest of the plateau region.

The landscape in the Simyen Mountains is dotted with lobelia trees and various scrub (stunted trees and shrubs).

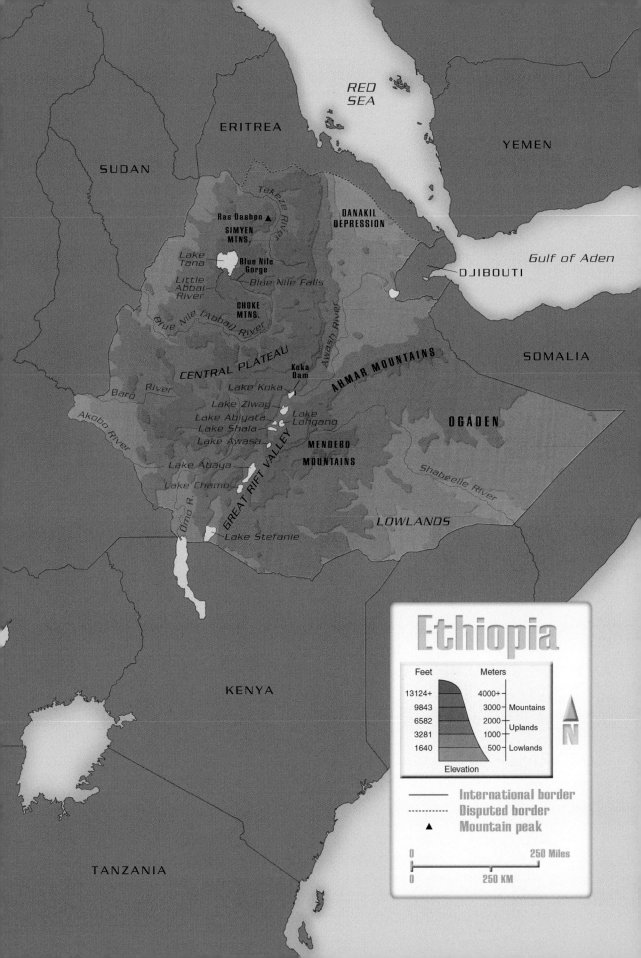

SUDAN

ERITREA

RED
SEA

YEMEN

Tekeze River

Ras Dashen ▲

SIMYEN
MTNS.

DANAKIL
DEPRESSION

Lake
Tana

Blue Nile
Gorge

Gulf of Aden

Little
Abbai
River

Blue Nile Falls

DJIBOUTI

CHOKE
MTNS.

Blue Nile (Abbai) River

Awash River

Baro   River

CENTRAL PLATEAU

Koka
Dam

AHMAR MOUNTAINS

SOMALIA

Lake Koka

Akoba River

Lake Ziway

Lake Abiyata

Lake
Lahgano

OGADEN

Lake Shala

Lake Awasa

Lake Abaya

MENDEBO

MOUNTAINS

Shabeelle River

Lake Chamo

GREAT RIFT VALLEY

Omo R.

Lake Stefanie

LOWLANDS

KENYA

TANZANIA

Ethiopia

Feet	Meters	
13124+	4000+	
9843	3000	Mountains
6582	2000	Uplands
3281	1000	
1640	500	Lowlands
Elevation		

N

──────── International border

--------- Disputed border

▲ Mountain peak

0 _____ 250 Miles

0 _____ 250 KM

The Choke Mountains, another major range, lie to the north and west of the capital city of Addis Ababa.

The Central Plateau continues east of the Great Rift Valley. It includes mountains, such as the Mendebo and Ahmar ranges, and a semiarid plain known as the Ogaden. Lower in elevation, the eastern plateau has been the scene of a long border dispute with Somalia, which hopes to acquire the Ogaden. This area is among the most vulnerable to drought and resulting famine.

THE GREAT RIFT VALLEY Stretching from the Middle East to southeastern Africa, the Great Rift Valley is a fault in the earth's crust that was formed by volcanic action or by earthquakes. In the southern portion of Ethiopia, the Great Rift Valley becomes a deep trench that cuts through the central plateau from northeast to southwest. This valley also includes the Danakil Depression, a large triangular desert that crosses the border between Ethiopia and Eritrea. Sections of the depression are 300 feet (91 m) below sea level and record some of the hottest temperatures in the world.

THE LOWLANDS With elevations of 3,000 feet (914 m) and lower, lowlands make up much of Ethiopia's borderlands. These areas have a much hotter and drier climate than the Central Plateau and the Great Rift Valley. Because of their harsh climate, which makes much of the land unsuitable for farming, Ethiopia's Lowlands are sparsely populated.

Rivers and Lakes

The Blue Nile, called the Abbai in Ethiopia, is the most notable of Ethiopia's rivers and the chief tributary (contributor) of the Nile River, the world's longest river. The Blue Nile originates in Lake Tana in northern Ethiopia and flows through the western section of the Central Plateau to join the White Nile in Khartoum, Sudan. The Blue Nile, the Tekeze, and the Baro, which all contribute to the Nile, account for about half of the outflow of water from Ethiopia. Other major rivers include the Awash, which flows into a series of small lakes in the Lowlands of the east, and the Shabeelle, which cuts through the southeastern portion of the country and goes into Somalia.

Lake Tana, the largest freshwater lake in Ethiopia, is situated on the Ethiopian Plateau. Roughly square in shape, the lake covers an area of about 1,100 square miles (2,849 sq. km). A chain of lakes—Koka, Ziway, Langano, Abiyata, Shala, Awasa, Abaya, Chamo, and Stefanie—lie close to one another in the Great Rift Valley. Some of

them are freshwater lakes and, therefore, are dependent on small rivers feeding into them. Others receive their large volume of water from hot, underground springs containing various salts and minerals.

Climate

Ethiopia lies entirely within the tropics, an area where the climate is warm year-round. Differences in elevation produce variations in temperature ranging from cool to temperate to hot. These variations are known to Ethiopians as *dega, weina dega,* and *kolla,* respectively.

The cool zone (dega) consists of the Central Plateau, which has elevations above 7,000 feet (2,134 m). Temperatures in this zone range from 60°F (16°C) to the freezing point. Summerlike temperatures occur during the months of March, April, and May.

THE BLUE NILE FALLS

Called Tis Isat ("Smoking Fire") or Tis Abbai ("Smoking Nile") by Ethiopians, the Blue Nile Falls *(above)* is one of the most spectacular waterfalls in Africa. Just after the rainy season, the falls often reach a width of 1,300 feet (400 m), sending millions of gallons of water over a sheer 150-foot (45-m) drop. The roar of the falls can be heard from miles away, and its spray can be felt from one mile (1.6 km) away. The crashing water creates so much humidity that a rainforest has grown in the area around it, complete with thick vegetation and exotic animals, such as monkeys and parrots.

DROUGHT AND FAMINE IN ETHIOPIA

Ethiopia's climate makes it very vulnerable to droughts. Most Ethiopian farmers do not have access to irrigation systems for watering their crops and so are completely dependent on rain. When the country's rainy seasons fail to provide enough moisture, as they have several times in recent decades, the results can be catastrophic. Since most Ethiopians are subsistence farmers—only able to grow enough food and raise enough livestock to feed themselves, as opposed to selling them—poor harvests often lead to famine.

Ethiopia suffered one of its worst famines in the mid-1980s, when two consecutive years of drought left millions of people starving. Tens of thousands died. A more severe drought began in 1999, lasting for four consecutive years. According to a United Nations World Food Program Report, about 7.3 million Ethiopians face food shortages in 2004. The UN and other aid organizations have provided millions of tons of food aid to the country in recent years. But solutions to the recurrent drought problem lie in developing irrigation systems that can provide water to crops when rain is scarce.

The temperate region (weina dega) is a pleasant place to live and a productive place to farm. This climatic zone covers much of Ethiopia's mountainous areas and is densely populated. Altitudes range from 5,000 to 7,000 feet (1,524 to 2,134 m), and temperatures average between 60°F (16°C) and 85°F (29°C).

The hot zone (kolla) includes the Danakil Depression and nearby Lowlands, the eastern Ogaden, and the deep valleys of the Blue Nile River. These regions are less than 5,000 feet (1,524 m) above sea level. The climatic conditions are uncomfortably hot throughout the year, and the temperature varies from 85°F (29°C) to as high as 122°F (50°C) in some places.

In addition to different climatic zones, Ethiopia has two identifiable seasons. The dry season occurs from mid-September through May, although a brief period of light rains, known as the *belg*, occurs from February to May. The rainiest season, called the *meher*, takes place during the months of June, July, and August. Average annual rainfall varies according to elevation, with higher areas generally being wetter. Addis Ababa, situated in the mountains, gets about 43 inches (109 centimeters) of rain per year. Rainfall is less in the Lowlands and in river valleys. Desert areas such as the Ogaden and parts of the Danakil Depression are the driest regions, receiving from 0 to 8 inches (20 cm) annually.

Flora and Fauna

During the twentieth century, Ethiopia—like most African nations—has encountered the problem of dwindling forests. Since the 1960s, the country has gone from being nearly 40 percent forested to less than 3 percent forested. The loss has been due to the use of large quantities of wood for both construction and fuel. In addition, major forest fires have devastated the country's woodlands. In many cases, farmers start these fires when clearing land to grow crops. On occasion these fires grow out of control and cause tremendous damage. For example, in early 2000, forest fires burned for more than three months, destroying more than 741,316 acres (300,000 hectares) of forest and cropland. A 2002 UN study concluded that Ethiopia's forests could be completely gone by 2020 if measures aren't taken to preserve them.

The loss of forests has created problems for the country's farmers. In the north and other semiarid areas, the desert is expanding, leaving less and less land suitable for cultivation. Moreover, the loss of trees has resulted in continual erosion of topsoil from heavy rainfall as well as from tropical winds.

Although minor efforts to reforest have begun, Ethiopia continues to struggle against the environmental problems that arise from deforestation. The Ethiopian government has declared that conservation and development of the nation's forests is a high priority. But no major policies and programs have been put into effect, due to a lack of financial resources.

Ethiopia's vegetation varies widely, from arid scrubland in the Danakil region to lush wetlands in the west and northwest.

The Lowlands along the international boundaries of the east and northeast are semidesert or desert regions, with little or no rain throughout the year. The terrain is dotted with bushy growth, interrupted only by an occasional acacia tree. A common plant is sansevieria, popular as a houseplant in Great Britain and the United States, where it is often called a snake plant.

Temperate-zone forests and high mountain vegetation cover Ethiopia's plateaus. Eucalyptus—a tree imported from Australia—grows around Addis Ababa and other cities. The tree's root system, which develops quickly and holds the soil together, helps to control erosion.

Ethiopia boasts a variety of wildlife, including most of the familiar African mammals—elephants, zebras, giraffes, lions, leopards, antelope, rhinoceroses, hyenas, and baboons. Hippopotamuses and crocodiles inhabit lakes and rivers, and reptiles and fish abound. In the Great Rift Valley, birds such as cuckoos, weaverbirds, hawks, eagles, flamingos, and flycatchers are plentiful. In the Simyen Mountains, walia ibex—mountain goats found only in Ethiopia—roam freely. The Ethiopian wolf is the rarest member of the canid

Two Ethiopian wolves play-fight in Bale Mountains National Park, home to more than half of Ethiopia's wolf population. The wolves have been critically endangered since 1974. To learn more about conservation efforts regarding Ethiopian wildlife, visit www.vgsbooks.com for links.

(dog) family in the world. Only a few hundred of these creatures remain, and they exist only in the Ethiopian highlands.

Natural Resources

The mineral resources of Ethiopia have not been fully investigated. So far, gold and platinum are the only metals of economic value that have been mined. Surveys made when Italy occupied the nation in the 1930s, as well as those made in recent years, indicate the presence of copper, lead, magnesium, and iron. Potash, a substance containing the element potassium, which is used for making fertilizers, soaps, detergents, ceramics, textiles, dyes, and chemicals, is available in the Danakil region. Deposits of clay and limestone are common, but they support only a modest amount of brick and cement manufacturing. Extensive salt deposits also exist, and recent studies indicate that petroleum deposits lie in the south. Ethiopia's mineral resources have not yet been exploited due to the country's rugged terrain and lack of infrastructure, such as roads, railways, power lines, and telephone lines.

With its many mountains and rivers, Ethiopia has great potential for generating hydroelectric power. Several plants are in operation along the Awash River, with the Koka Dam being the largest. Surveyors have also noted the Danakil region's potential for harnessing geothermal power (using the heat of the earth's interior), and efforts are under way to tap this resource.

Cities

Only 15 percent of Ethiopia's total population reside in urban areas. The rest live in rural parts of the country, although famine and civil strife have caused more rural inhabitants to move to the cities.

THE CIVET CAT

Ethiopia's civet cat is not really a cat at all but a member of the mongoose family. A mammal with long, gray hair and spots and bands on its back, it was once a highly sought-after commercial commodity. The civet cat has glands near its tail, where a musky substance, similar to that found in a skunk, is produced. This substance, called civet, has an unpleasant smell but was highly prized as an ingredient in the making of perfumes because it captures and retains delicate fragrances. Civet was usually harvested by capturing and confining the cats and then extracting the civet through a process that was painful to the animal. Ethiopia was once a key supplier of civet, but in recent years, the product is in less demand due to synthetic replacement substances.

ADDIS ABABA Addis Ababa means "new flower" in the Ethiopian language of Amharic, and the city was founded in 1886 by Sahle Mariam, the man who would become Emperor Menelik II. The capital of Ethiopia since 1896, it is the headquarters of the United Nations Economic Commission for Africa. Addis Ababa's Africa Hall is the seat of the African Union (formerly the Organization of African States), an organization of African countries that works for better cooperation among African states.

Broad avenues crisscross the sprawling capital, which has a population of more than 4 million people. The city is 8,200 feet (2,500 m) above sea level, which gives it a springlike climate throughout the year. Modern buildings stand side by side with traditional mud homes, and the city's Merkato is the largest open-air market in eastern Africa.

SECONDARY URBAN CENTERS Other important urban centers are scattered throughout the country. Dire Dawa (population 208,000) is Ethiopia's second largest city. It was founded in 1902 as a station for the country's only railway line. From the seventeenth to the nineteenth

Although **Addis Ababa** is a bustling urban center of more than 4 million people, Ethiopia's cities are home to only 15 percent of the country's population. For more information about Ethiopia's cities, including what there is to see and do in each city, what the weather is like there, and more, visit www.vgsbooks.com for links.

centuries, Gonder (population 142,000)—located about 20 miles (32 km) north of Lake Tana—was Ethiopia's capital. During the reigns of the seventeenth-century emperor Fasilides and his successors, many castles, palaces, and fortifications were built. Gonder has not only castles, but also beautiful churches, which managed to survive the destruction of several invading armies. Dese, the capital of Welo Province in north-central Ethiopia, has a population of about 123,000. In the primarily Muslim southeastern region lies Harer (population 122,000), which is in an important coffee-growing region. Debre Markos (population 49,300), the capital of the Gojam Province, is situated about 110 miles (177 km) northwest of Addis Ababa.

Aksum (population 27,000) was an imperial city in the early Christian era during the height of the Aksumite kingdom. Crowning ceremonies of Ethiopian emperors took place in Aksum until the Middle Ages. Beautiful tombs, some of which are giant stelae (upright stone slabs), mark the remains of ancient kings. Ancient peoples believed that the stelae represented the gateway through which the soul of the deceased person traveled to the afterworld. The remains of Aksum's rich past make it a popular destination for tourists.

HISTORY AND GOVERNMENT

Archaeological findings reveal that ancestors of *Homo sapiens* lived in Ethiopia about four million years ago. The known history of Ethiopia began when Sabaeans from Sheba, a kingdom in southern Arabia, crossed the Red Sea sometime between 2000 and 1000 B.C.

The Sabaeans spoke Semitic languages, early forms of the languages that became modern Arabic, Hebrew, and several Ethiopian languages, such as Amharic and Tigrinya. Settling along the coast, the Sabaeans eventually moved inland to the highlands of modern-day Tigray Province and Eritrea in eastern Ethiopia, where they came into contact with the Cushitic speakers who already lived in the area. A mixed Semitic-Cushitic people emerged from this mingling.

Legend has it that in the tenth century B.C., the ruler of these peoples, Maqueda, the queen of Sheba, decided to lead an expedition to the court of King Solomon of Israel. An inexperienced ruler, she hoped the king would teach her how to be an effective monarch. Attracted by her beauty, the king tricked the queen into a sexual

encounter, which produced a child. The child ascended the throne of his mother as Menelik I. Thus, according to tradition, he became the first of a long line of Ethiopian emperors descended from Solomon.

The Aksumite Kingdom

By the first century A.D., this dynasty (family of rulers) ruled a kingdom whose capital was at Aksum. At its height, from the fourth to the seventh centuries A.D., the Aksumite kingdom covered most of modern-day Eritrea, Tigray Province, and Welo Province. In Adulis, Aksum's port on the Red Sea, Egyptian sailors, Syrian traders, and East Indian merchants bartered for gold, copper, utensils, olive oil, and spices. Aksum also conducted a brisk trade in ivory and rhinoceros horns.

Along with goods, some Middle Eastern traders brought a new kind of religion to Ethiopia—Christianity. Missionaries from Syria converted the Aksumite king Ezana to Christianity in the fourth century. Eventually, the king's subjects also adopted the new religion.

Christianity influenced the development of religious art, music, and literature. The latter was written in Geez, which is still used in Ethiopian Christian rites and is the forerunner of modern Ethiopian languages.

LALIBELA

Each year, thousands of Christians flock to the town of Lalibela in northern Ethiopia, where they celebrate Christian holidays in Lalibela's eleven sacred rock churches *(below)*. These spectacular houses of worship were not built but, in fact, were carved out of the region's rocklike sculptures. The town is named after Lalibela, the twelfth-century king who founded it and commissioned the building of the churches.

The power of the Aksumite kingdom began to wane in the seventh century, as armies of Arabs—who followed the faith of Islam and were called Muslims—gained control of Arabia, the Red Sea, and northern Africa. This trend ended the long cultural contact between Christian countries and Ethiopia. Thereafter, Ethiopia was cut off from the rest of the Christian world by Muslim territory. As a result, the kingdom's trade with Europe largely ended.

Pushed out of northern Ethiopia by Muslim armies, the Aksumite kingdom tried to reestablish itself farther south. It failed to acquire small kingdoms in the heartland of present-day Ethiopia and to convert the peoples there to Christianity. Meanwhile, the Muslim armies were again on the move. By the tenth century, the Aksumite kingdom had lost all its land to Muslim conquest.

◉ Return of the Solomonic Line

In the 1130s, a new line of Christian kings—the Zagwe—established itself in Ethiopia. A Cushitic people, the Zagwe came from modern-day Welo Province. They founded their capital at Roha (modern-day Lalibela) and dotted the landscape there with churches and monasteries. Unlike the Aksumite kingdom, the Zagwe dynasty could not claim royal descent from Solomon and Sheba (called the Solomonic line). The Ethiopian Orthodox Church, along with remnants—such as the Amhara and the Tigray peoples—of the former Aksumite kingdom came to regard a connection with the Solomonic line as the only legitimate link to the Ethiopian throne.

In 1270 Yekuno Amlaq, an Amhara prince who claimed to be a descendant of the Solomonic line, overthrew the Zagwe and reestablished the Solomonic dynasty. The center of the reborn kingdom was in modern-day northern Ethiopia. Yekuno Amlaq and his successors extended this region to include many Muslim territories, such as Gojam and Gonder in the northwestern part of modern-day Ethiopia. Zera Yaqob, a ruthless though efficient Ethiopian king, ruled from 1434 to 1468. Militarily, he managed to defeat or limit the power of smaller, surrounding realms. Zera Yaqob also tried to spread Christianity to previously non-Christian areas in the region and encouraged the spread of Geez literature, writing several religious works himself.

ETHIOPIA'S NAMES

The name *Ethiopia* comes from a Greek term, *Aithiopia*, which roughly means "land of the burnt faces." In ancient times, Greek travelers made many trips to the Horn of Africa, returning to their homeland with tales of beautiful, dark-skinned people and exotic animals. Aksumite kings, when writing in Greek, used this name when referring to their country. In modern times, Ethiopians refer to their country as Ethiopia. The local spelling is Ityop'iya.

The name *Abyssinia*, long used by Europeans to denote Ethiopia, dates from the 1500s. The word is a variation of *al-Habesha*, the name of an area near the coast of the Red Sea.

More Muslim Invaders

A series of short-lived and ineffective rulers followed Zera Yaqob. As a result, the central government became less effective at collecting taxes and funding its military. This weakness left Christian Ethiopia vulnerable to another wave of Muslim invasions.

Raids and counterraids went on between Christians and Muslims until the leader of the Muslim armies, Ahmad ibn Ibrahim al-Ghazi, waged a jihad (holy war) to break Christian rule in Ethiopia. A popular military chief and strong religious leader, al-Ghazi attracted a large following. In 1529 his Muslim forces dramatically defeated the Christian troops of the Ethiopian emperor Lebna Dengel. The victors took prisoners, burned churches, and continued to march toward the interior. Eventually, they penetrated the heartland of the Ethiopian Empire—modern-day northern Ethiopia.

Lebna Dengel died in 1540. His successor, Gelawdewos, sought allies to help him fight al-Ghazi's forces. In 1541 the European nation of Portugal sent troops armed with modern weapons to assist the Ethiopian emperor. With help from the Portuguese soldiers, Gelawdewos's forces began driving al-Ghazi back. In turn, al-Ghazi turned to the Ottoman Empire (a large Muslim empire based in modern-day Turkey) for military support. Years of bitter fighting followed until in 1543 the two leaders' forces met in a climactic battle. Al-Ghazi was killed and his army fled. This event was a permanent blow to Muslim power in Ethiopia. And although Gelawdewos could claim victory, the long period of warfare, which had left hundreds of thousands dead, permanently weakened the Christian empire. Meanwhile, the contact with Europe opened doors and shifted Ethiopia from a period of isolation to one of participation in the world scene.

Contact with Europe

Following the Muslim defeat, relations with Portugal were strained by the activities of Portuguese and Spanish missionaries. These Europeans traveled south to convert Ethiopians from their traditional form of Christianity, the Ethiopian Orthodox Church, to Roman Catholicism. In the early seventeenth century, Emperor Za Dengel secretly converted to Catholicism. When this change was made public, the kingdom's provincial lords (wealthy landowners) were outraged. Za Dengel was removed from power and replaced by his Orthodox grandson, Susenyos. Yet Susenyos sought to expand the empire through a military alliance with the Europeans. To help achieve this goal and win over the Spanish and Portuguese, he too, converted to Catholicism. Roman Catholic priests ordered the removal of Orthodox priests, and changed religious teachings and the schedule of holidays and festivals. Angered by this threat to their traditional religion, many Ethiopians revolted.

With the kingdom on the verge of civil war, Susenyos stepped down in 1632. His Orthodox son Fasilides came to power and soon expelled the Catholic missionaries. Thereafter, Ethiopia maintained a more distant political relationship with Europe. But the kingdom continued to strengthen ties with the outside world through trade. In particular, demand for Ethiopian coffee created a network of trade with Europe and the Middle East.

Internally, the Solomonic dynasty, weakened by internal struggles, fought a losing battle to maintain control over its realm. This led to a period known as the Era of the Princes, which began in the mid-1700s and lasted for nearly one hundred years. The emperor's centralized authority gave way to the power of independent regional rulers, each of whom controlled a specific area. Civil wars were common during this chaotic period.

Tewodros II

Among the warring princes was Kassa Hailu, a strong military leader who succeeded in establishing his power over most of the country. He was crowned emperor in 1855, taking the name of Tewodros II. He worked to reunify the country under his rule by taking control of churches and armies that had previously been locally run institutions. But these changes, which led to higher taxes and cries of protest from church leaders, made Tewodros unpopular.

Meanwhile, another ruler, Sahle Mariam, king of the Shewa Province in central Ethiopia, had been heir to the Ethiopian throne when Tewodros took it. The new emperor put the heir in prison, but Sahle Mariam escaped in 1865 and joined a rebel group that actively opposed the Tewodros regime.

In need of military allies to support his threatened rule, Tewodros looked to Great Britain for help. When his requests were ignored, Tewodros angrily imprisoned several British citizens who were visiting his court, accusing them of plotting against him. As a result, the British sent troops to Ethiopia in 1868. The rebels joined the British, and in the battle that followed, Tewodros was defeated, after which he took his own life.

Disorder prevailed until 1872, when the ruler of Tigray Province proclaimed himself Emperor John IV. The new ruler also sought to unify the country under his leadership, but he was soon

John IV aided the British in their campaign against Tewodros. In return, the British supplied John with money and weapons, which he used to gain the throne.

faced with several external threats. The first came from the Muslim nation of Egypt. Troops from that country were moving in from the north, seizing Ethiopia's Red Sea ports with the intention of making Ethiopia an Egyptian colony. In 1876 John IV led a huge army against the Egyptians, driving them out of the region. The emperor's successful leadership against the invaders made him highly popular. John IV used his newfound strength to bring several kingdoms of the region under his control. But more threats remained, including Sahle Mariam.

Sahle Mariam had reclaimed control of the Shewa kingdom. Taking the name Menelik, he remained independent and refused to recognize John IV as emperor. In 1882 another external power—the Italians—forced the emperor on the defensive, seizing a Red Sea port and invading northern Ethiopia. John IV's forces defeated the invading Italians, but another threat was looming to the west.

A group of Muslims from the Sudan, known as Mahdists, attacked the empire from the west. In 1889 John IV led an army against the Mahdist invaders. The Mahdists defeated the Ethiopians, and John IV was killed. That year, with his main rival gone, Menelik of Shewa successfully claimed the throne as Menelik II.

⊙ Menelik II

Through military victories and alliances, Menelik II was able to expand the borders of the Ethiopian Empire to nearly double their original size. He also established the new capital of his empire at Addis Ababa and began construction of a railroad that would link the capital and Djibouti. During this period, however, the empire lost its access to the sea when Italy seized Eritrea.

Like other European powers in the late nineteenth century, Italy was determined to secure territories in Africa. The Italians focused their colonial desires on northeastern Africa, particularly on Ethiopia. Hoping to avoid another invasion, Menelik negotiated the Treaty of Wichale, granting Italy the right to hold Eritrea. The Italians prepared two copies of the treaty, one in Amharic—the Ethiopian language—and the other in Italian. On the strength of the Italian version, Francesco Crispi, the prime minister of Italy, made it known to all European countries that Ethiopia had been made a protectorate (dependent political unit) of Italy. The European powers adjusted their maps accordingly.

When Menelik II discovered the misunderstanding, he protested immediately. The wording of the treaty in Amharic gave the emperor the right to ask for help from Italy in times of need, but the treaty did not make Ethiopia a territory of Italy. Menelik II at once wrote to

Britain's Queen Victoria, to the ruler of Germany, and to the president of France, insisting that Ethiopia was still an independent nation. The European rulers ignored his claims, and in 1893 Menelik denounced the treaty. By 1895 Ethiopia and Italy were at war.

In March 1896, Menelik's troops soundly defeated an Italian army of about 15,000 soldiers at Adwa. Italy later negotiated a new treaty, in which Italy recognized Ethiopia's independence but retained control of Eritrea.

The Early Twentieth Century

Menelik died in 1913. Lij Ayasu, his grandson and successor, was a weak ruler who soon angered the country's nobles (wealthy landowners). When Ayasu sought to ally his country with his Muslim neighbors, the Christian nobles deposed him in 1916. Thereafter, Menelik's daughter Zauditu ruled as empress. Her cousin Ras Tafari, Menelik's grandnephew, was proclaimed Zauditu's heir, successor, and regent (one who governs for a monarch).

Ras Tafari quickly overshadowed Zauditu, beginning a program to further modernize the country, introducing European legal codes, and encouraging trade with Europe. In 1923 he earned his country a place on the international

MODERNIZATION UNDER MENELIK

During his twenty-four-year reign, Menelik *(above)* began many programs to modernize Ethiopia. In addition to the construction of the country's first (and only) railway, he also commissioned the building of bridges and roads and oversaw the establishment of postal, telephone, and telegraph services. In addition, Menelik encouraged the importing of modern manufactured goods, such as clothing and agricultural tools.

stage by gaining a seat in the League of Nations, an international organization created to maintain peace between nations. Five years later, he signed a treaty of friendship with Italy that allowed Ethiopia free access to Italy's Eritrean ports. The empress died in 1930, and on November 2 of that year, Ras Tafari was crowned emperor under the name Haile Selassie.

Haile Selassie claimed to be the 225th successor of the Solomonic dynasty. Haile Selassie's official titles included "king of kings" and "the lion of Judah." Seven months after his ascension to the throne, the emperor decreed the nation's first written constitution. The document provided for a local and national legislature (lawmaking body), but power over the country's government, courts, and military still rested with the emperor. He also ordered an ambitious road-building program to link the country's major cities, created a public school system in Addis Ababa, and imported printing presses for the purpose of creating national newspapers. But a second Italian invasion cut short Haile Selassie's reforms.

Visit www.vgsbooks.com to find links to resources on the second Italian invasion of Ethiopia, Ethiopia's involvement in World War II, and the rise of Haile Selassie.

The Second Italian Invasion and Postwar Rule

Despite the signing of several treaties, the border between Ethiopia and Italy's colonies in Eritrea and Somalia remained in

Though the constitution Ethiopia adopted under **Haile Selassie** provided new legislatures, it also granted the new emperor nearly absolute power and declared his body sacred.

Italian troops march across northern Ethiopia in November 1935. The towns they marched through quickly surrendered to the invading troops.

dispute. Italian dictator Benito Mussolini, eager to expand Italian power, used the dispute to provoke a war with Ethiopia. Late in 1934, shots were exchanged across the border. In October 1935, Italian troops invaded Ethiopia, conquering the entire country in seven months.

Haile Selassie fled Ethiopia. In a speech before the League of Nations, he pleaded for assistance against the Italians. His pleas were ignored, and both France and Great Britain—which wanted to avoid conflicts that might lead to war—recognized Italy's control of Ethiopia. In addition, the league voted not to impose any penalties on Italy. The only major powers who refused to acknowledge Italy's position were the United States and the Soviet Union.

In 1939 World War II (1939–1945) began. Great Britain fought against Italy in this conflict. As a result, British and Ethiopian troops invaded Ethiopia, overthrowing the Italian forces. Arriving in Addis Ababa in 1941, exactly five years after he had left the capital, Haile Selassie soon regained authority throughout most of the nation. Following the end of the war, the emperor made his country one of the founding members of the United Nations, an international peacekeeping organization.

During the postwar years, loans from the United States provided funds to build roads, factories, and schools. By the 1950s, a thriving coffee trade also provided additional government revenue. In Europe and the United States, Haile Selassie was admired as a modern and forward-thinking ruler.

Yet these changes produced only modest progress, and the era of modernization stagnated in the mid-1950s. At that time, Latin American coffee producers began to flood the international market, lowering the price of Ethiopia's chief export. Drought and resulting famine struck rural areas, further slowing the development process.

Haile Selassie's attempts to modernize did not include reforming the nation's political structure. Throughout his reign, government officials were hired based on their loyalty to the emperor, not because of their qualifications. As a result, an inefficient bureaucracy developed that did little to help the needs of ordinary Ethiopians. At the same time, a new generation of younger Ethiopians, eager to reform the government, was organizing and preparing plans to stage a coup, or overthrow, of the emperor.

In 1960, while Haile Selassie was abroad, a group of revolutionaries declared a coup. Large numbers of university students supported the takeover. Despite its popular goals, the coup attempt collapsed—mainly because the country's army and air force remained loyal to the emperor. Unprepared to wage war against Ethiopia's military, the coup plotters quickly surrendered. Nevertheless, the coup shattered the view that the monarch was universally accepted.

In the previous decade, the United Nations had made Eritrea part of Ethiopia. Ethiopia claimed Eritrea as a province—to be administered by the central Ethiopian government. Yet the Eritreans never accepted rule by Ethiopia, and the situation led to a guerrilla war. Groups of Eritrean fighters clashed with Ethiopian armed forces throughout the 1960s.

At about the same time, Somalia declared its independence in 1960. The new Somali government soon announced its desire to make the Ogaden in southern Ethiopia—an area with a large Somali population—a part of the new Somalia. In 1963 a guerrilla war broke out, with Somali rebels attacking Ethiopian police stations and military bases in the region. The Somali army supported the rebels, providing them with arms and equipment.

The Fall of Haile Selassie

In addition to these outside threats, signs of internal dissatisfaction with the monarchy became more apparent by the late 1960s and early 1970s. A growing number of Ethiopians began to protest against the government, which they felt worked in the interest of the wealthy landowners at the expense of poor citizens. Many of these protesters held socialist views, believing that the country's land and industries should belong to the government instead of a small group of wealthy nobles.

In the early 1970s, another famine spread across northern and eastern Ethiopia. Because the emperor feared that the disaster might damage his reputation overseas, he chose not to tell the international community about the ravaging starvation in his realm. As a result, 300,000 people died of famine in eleven regions. Not until November 1973 did the emperor allow international agencies to engage in emergency relief operations. The emperor's mishandling of the famine, coupled with other economic disasters, led to strikes and protests throughout the country. That same year, another antigovernment group, the Oromo Liberation Front (OLF), established itself and called for an independent nation for the Oromo people in southern Ethiopia.

By early 1974, Haile Selassie had lost the support of not only the general public, but also the military. In June a group of officers formed a *derg*—meaning "committee" in Amharic—and plotted the overthrow of the emperor. A few months later, in September 1974, the Derg took control of the government and abolished the monarchy. After forty-four years of complete power, Emperor Haile Selassie was driven out of the palace grounds in an old Volkswagen. Soon after, Haile Selassie was murdered while in the custody of the new government. Dozens of members of the old regime were also executed.

Late in 1974, the Derg declared Ethiopia a socialist state. In the coming months, all industries, banks, and farms were nationalized—taken from their private owners and made the property of the government. Within a few years, Major (later Lieutenant Colonel) Mengistu Haile-Mariam emerged as the leader of the government. Holding strong

Haile Selassie's undemocratic rule led to widespread protests in the early 1970s.

socialist beliefs, Mengistu turned away from the West and sought to ally Ethiopia with Communist countries, such as the Soviet Union and Cuba, receiving financial and military aid from these countries.

Armed with Soviet weapons, Mengistu's forces fought off a Somali invasion of the Ogaden in the late-1970s. The Ethiopian military also scored a series of victories against guerrilla forces in Eritrea. At the same time, Mengistu's regime steadily became more authoritarian, stamping out political opposition and eliminating public dissent (criticism of the government). Thousands of dissenting Ethiopians were either executed or fled the country.

The Politics of Famine

Mengistu's regime nationalized the country's land in order to collectivize Ethiopia's agriculture. This meant that communities or groups, instead of individuals or families, owned the country's farms. Earnings from agriculture went to the group, not the individual. With little personal stake in their farms, many farmers had few incentives to work hard to get the most from their land. Several poor harvests left little surplus grain in case of an emergency. Then, in 1983, another drought struck the country. A disastrous famine followed the next year.

At first, the Mengistu regime refused to acknowledge the extent of the crisis, ignoring reports in the international media. As a result, tens of

A woman holds a malnourished child at a camp for Ethiopian famine victims in Danan. An estimated six Ethiopian children die per day from famine, while nearly seven million Ethiopians need famine relief because of widespread drought and poor crop yields. To learn more about the famine in Ethiopia and international relief efforts, visit www.vgsbooks.com for links.

thousands of Ethiopians died of hunger during the summer of 1984. By fall the regime could no longer deny the situation and began to seek international help. This included the efforts of worldwide money-raising campaigns such as Live Aid and USA for Africa. Nevertheless, Ethiopian officials hampered the efforts of international agencies to deliver relief supplies, especially to war-torn areas of northern Ethiopia such as Eritrea and Tigray. In 1987 Eritrea guerrillas destroyed trucks and food supplies that were on their way to relief camps in the region.

In an attempt to avoid future famines, the Mengistu government began a resettlement program aimed at relocating refugees into the more fertile areas of the country, particularly in the south. These areas were less affected by famine and had better agricultural potential. The program's goal was to resettle 30 million rural people into villages

LIVE AID FOR ETHIOPIA

In July 1985, during the height of an Ethiopian famine, many of the world's most popular musicians gathered to stage a concert to raise money to help Ethiopia's starving population. The event, called Live Aid, was held simultaneously in two stadiums—in London, England, and in Philadelphia, Pennsylvania *(above)*—with the entire concert broadcast on television across the globe. For sixteen hours, musical acts such as U2, Madonna, Ozzy Osbourne and Black Sabbath, Elton John, Led Zeppelin, and many others played their music and urged a worldwide audience to donate funds to help the people of Ethiopia. The hugely successful event raised more than $100 million for famine relief.

made up of collectivized farms. Yet these fertile areas lacked food, housing, farming equipment, and medical resources. Citizens were forced to move, often against their will. Of 600,000 refugees who were forcibly relocated in 1986, about 100,000 died of disease and starvation en route to the new areas. The deeply unpopular program created widespread anger against the Mengistu regime. Many citizens took up arms against the government.

Overthrow of Mengistu

By the late 1980s, the Mengistu regime was on the verge of collapse. Eritrean rebels had joined forces with an independence movement in the northern province of Tigray and driven government forces out of much of Eritrea and Tigray. Antigovernment Tigrayans, Eritreans, and others formed the Ethiopian People's Revolutionary Democratic Front (EPRDF) to bring down Mengistu. Meanwhile, huge expenditures on arms had left the Ethiopian government nearly bankrupt.

Rebel attacks intensified, and by May 1991, antigovernment forces had taken control of much of the northern half of the country. As the rebel

Rebel tanks flood the streets of Addis Ababa on May 30, 1991, following Mengistu's fall from power.

army advanced on Addis Ababa, Mengistu fled the capital. Meles Zenawi, the leader of the EPRDF, became Ethiopia's provisional (temporary) president.

Zenawi arranged a conference in July, and many rebel groups sent representatives. The conference established an interim government and planned nationwide, free elections. A new legislature, made up of several rival political groups, began meeting in Addis Ababa.

The defeat of Mengistu encouraged the independence movement in Eritrea, which was no longer opposed by the Ethiopian army. In the spring of 1993, the Eritreans voted overwhelmingly for self-rule. The United Nations quickly recognized the province as an independent country, but the exact border between the two countries remained in dispute.

A New Beginning

In Ethiopia, elections were held in the summer of 1995, with the EPRDF winning an overwhelming majority. Zenawi became Ethiopia's prime minister. In 1996 a new government replaced the provisional government, and the country assumed a new name—the Federal Democratic Republic of Ethiopia. The Ethiopian economy began to recover from years of war, with several foreign nations investing directly in Ethiopian businesses. But a new war halted much of this development.

In May 1998, Ethiopia and Eritrea went to war over their contested border, clashing over a small piece of disputed land. The conflict lasted for more than two years, during which about 100,000 soldiers were killed. A peace agreement was signed in June 2000, but the border issue was still not resolved to the satisfaction of both governments. Representatives from the UN, United States, Europe, and other African countries have pressed the two countries to come to an agreement. But in early 2004, the issue had not been resolved, and each side accused the other of being uncooperative. The threat of renewed hostilities remains.

Adding to Ethiopia's challenges, drought and famine have again ravaged the country in recent years. Four straight years of inadequate rainfall—from 1999 through 2002—resulted in another deadly famine. About 14 million Ethiopians suffered from inadequate amounts of food in 2003. International agencies worked around the clock to deliver food aid to Ethiopia's stricken population. But a strong harvest in late 2003 has helped bring some relief. In 2004 the number of Ethiopians needing food aid has been halved.

A woman sits in front of the ruins of her town, which is located on the border of Ethiopia and Eritrea. Like many other Ethiopian towns, it was badly damaged during the war with Eritrea.

Government

The Constitution of the Federal Democratic Republic of Ethiopia was adopted in December 1994. It established two universally elected representative bodies for the federal government—the House of People's Representatives and the House of Federation. Of the two bodies, the House of People's Representatives—which can number up to 550 members—is the sole federal lawmaking institution, while the 108-seat House of Federation's role is to interpret the Constitution and protect the rights of all citizens of Ethiopia. All of Ethiopia's peoples, nations, and ethnic groups are represented in the House of Federation. Members of each body serve five-year terms.

The House of People's Representatives elects a president to serve as Ethiopia's head of state. The president's role is largely ceremonial, and includes appointing ambassadors and high military titles. The highest executive powers belong to the prime minister, who heads a cabinet of sixteen officials who run the various government ministries. In local matters, district councils and neighborhood committees make decisions.

The Federal Supreme Court sits in Addis Ababa and is divided into civil, criminal, and military sections. A high court hears appeals on civil and criminal cases from provincial courts, which include *awraja* (regional) and *warada* (local) courts.

THE PEOPLE

According to the Population Reference Bureau, Ethiopia has a population of 70.7 million, making it the seventeenth largest country in the world. With a current growth rate of 2.7 percent, the country's population is projected to reach 117.6 million by 2025 and 173.3 million by 2050. Should these predictions hold true, Ethiopia will be the tenth most populated country in the world by 2050. As a nation that has frequently struggled to produce enough food to feed itself, such a rapid rise in population is cause for concern and makes the government's attempts to wipe out famine and to improve health care even more pressing.

In terms of income, Ethiopians have the lowest standard of living in the world. The average Ethiopian income is about $92 per year. Ethiopia's social programs rely heavily on foreign aid donations, of which the country receives about $900 million annually.

◉ Language and Ethnic Mixture

About 80 different ethnic groups live in Ethiopia. They are usually

classified according to the languages they speak, and thus more than 80 different languages are spoken in the country. Some languages are spoken by millions of Ethiopians, while others are spoken by just a few hundred. In turn, many of these languages can be further divided by dialect, making a total of more than 200 unique dialects in the country. Ethiopia's languages are generally organized into four main groups: Semitic, Cushitic, Omotic, and Nilo-Saharan.

Semitic languages are related to Hebrew and Arabic and are spoken primarily in the northern and central parts of the country. Amharic, the official language of Ethiopia, is a Semitic language. It is used in most government, academic, and business communication, and most modern Ethiopian literature is written in Amharic. Other Semitic languages include Tigrinya, which is spoken mainly in the Tigray Province, and Geez, the language of the ancient Aksumite kingdom. Geez, also known as Ethiopic, is not commonly spoken by the general population but remains the language of the Ethiopian Orthodox Church.

The related languages of Amharic, Tigrinya, and Geez use a set of characters handed down from the ancient languages of Arabia, with 31 basic characters that can be combined in different ways to make up more than 200 additional characters.

Cushitic languages are spoken mainly in Ethiopia's southern and eastern regions. Cushitic languages include Oromiffa, the language of the Oromo, as well as the Somali language, and the language of the Afar people. Far fewer Ethiopians speak Omotic languages. Those who do, including the Bana, Ari, and Karo peoples, usually live in the southwest, in the general area of the Omo River. Fewer than 2 percent of Ethiopians speak Nilo-Saharan languages, which are most prevalent in western Ethiopia along the border with Sudan.

As in many nations, the ethnic groups of Ethiopia are sometimes in conflict. Regional wars have been fought over land, religion, and the desire to acquire or maintain political power. In recent years, however, the struggle has shifted its focus to liberation from the political and economic domination of the Amharic- and Tigrinya-speaking groups. These peoples historically have been the most powerful ethnic communities in the country.

Making up between 32 to 50 percent of the population, the Oromo people are Ethiopia's largest ethnic group. Most Oromo live in the western, southern, and southeastern parts of the country. Although categorized by a similar language, the Oromo are a diverse group, with a variety of lifestyles. Some are pastoralists (shepherds, herders), while others are plow cultivators. Many practice mixed farming (crops and livestock). Some Oromo practice

Oromo men and women travel to the market. To learn more about Ethiopia's indigenous populations, visit www.vgsbooks.com for links.

Children under the age of fifteen account for nearly 45 percent of Ethiopia's population. These children are from Aweday, a small town between Dire Dawa and Harer.

traditional religions, while others are members of the Ethiopian Orthodox Church. Historically, the Oromo have struggled to receive fair treatment from the Amhara-dominated Ethiopian government. In response, some Oromo support an independent country for the Oromo people. The Oromo Liberation Front (OLF) has been engaged in an intermittent guerrilla war against the Ethiopian government since 1973.

The Amhara make up Ethiopia's second largest ethnic group, comprising about 30 percent of the population. The Amhara were the ruling group during Ethiopia's imperial era and still play a key role in the country's politics. Most Amhara are farmers and pastoralists, and the majority of them belong to the Ethiopian Orthodox Church.

The Tigray people of the north comprise approximately 6 percent of the Ethiopian population. Descendants of the ancient Aksumite kingdom, the Tigray are mostly farmers. Members of the Tigray group, including Prime Minister Meles Zenawi, dominate Ethiopia's ruling political party, the EPRDF. Other ethnic groups make up the rest of Ethiopia's population. They include the Gurage, who live in lowland areas, the Somali of the Ogaden, and the Danakil and Falasha, who live in several areas of the country.

◉ Health

Health care in Ethiopia is a powerful reminder of the country's need for development. Life expectancy is 42 years, and infant mortality

Collecting water is traditionally the job of women. In most rural areas, a lack of infrastructure means they have to travel far to collect water in large jugs. To learn more about the importance of water in Ethiopia and the role of women in Ethiopian society, visit www.vgsbooks.com for links.

is 107 deaths in every 1,000 live births. (The average for Africa as a whole is 88 per 1,000.) Ethiopia's health problems will require intensive efforts to wipe out diseases such as malaria, tuberculosis, and other ailments related to a lack of basic sanitation facilities. Some 80 percent of illnesses in the country are related to a lack of clean water, and only 24 percent of the population have access to safe drinking water. Most of these people live in urban areas. Among rural inhabitants, only 12 percent have access to safe drinking water.

Government efforts in the area of preventive health care have shown some results. People in rural areas have been educated about sanitary care, about the preservation of food, and about protecting their wells from contamination. But the country has too few hospitals and health clinics to serve its citizens adequately. The government sets aside about 5 percent of the national budget for health care, but much of the money for this service comes from foreign sources.

Recurring famine remains the greatest threat to Ethiopia's population. In particularly hard-hit regions, people may have to walk several miles to find water. As crops fail, farmers are often forced to sell off their livestock before it dies of starvation. Having sold off a source of food and their only commodity, many farmers are faced with starvation if the drought continues.

Beyond the threat of starvation, famine also threatens people by leaving them malnourished and weakened and thus more vulnerable to disease. In the 2000s, millions of Ethiopians are dependent on international food aid for survival. In addition to poor rains in many parts of the country, other factors have contributed to ongoing famine crisis. Lack of paved roads makes the transportation of supplies such as seed and fertilizer difficult and expensive. Moreover, transporting any leftover crops to market is equally challenging and unprofitable for farmers. In this continuing cycle, farmers cannot afford to purchase fertilizer or build irrigation systems.

In 2003 the Ethiopian government unveiled an ambitious plan to tackle the country's chronic famine. The plan involves improving roads, giving farmers access to better agricultural equipment, improving health and nutrition among rural citizens, and a voluntary resettlement scheme that will move farmers from drought-prone areas to more fertile locations. The program has received praise from the United Nations and foreign governments but will require billions of dollars in international aid to succeed.

Another serious threat to Ethiopia's population is the human immunodeficiency virus (HIV), the virus that causes the deadly disease acquired immunodeficiency syndrome (AIDS). An estimated 10 percent of Ethiopians carry the disease. Progress in fighting the spread of HIV/AIDS is hampered by a lack of resources to provide effective education and prevention programs, combined with a lack of medical facilities for treatment, and lack of funding for anti-HIV/AIDS drugs for citizens.

◉ Education

Ethiopia's development challenge is also clear in the area of education. The Ethiopian government has placed great emphasis on education as a way to provide young people with modern training for work in the nation's government and industries.

Before the twentieth century, the country's only source of education was the Ethiopian Orthodox Church, which trained people for religious duties and also educated the children of wealthy nobles. Students came mainly from the Central Plateau.

Ethiopia's first public school was established in Addis Ababa in 1907. But only a handful of students were enrolled, with the goal of training them to join the royal bureaucracy. The public school system grew slowly throughout Haile Selassie's reign, and by the 1950s, the country had about 400 schools. Ethiopia's first university, Haile Selassie I University, was

In 1975 the Derg temporarily closed Ethiopia's colleges and secondary schools for the purpose of sending sixty thousand students, teachers, and public school officials to the rural areas of the country. These students and professionals embarked on the Development through Cooperation Campaign—known to Ethiopians as the *zemecha* (campaign). The zemecha's goal was to promote the ideas of the newly declared socialist state, to organize land reform, and to help improve literacy rates and health care.

founded in 1961. But these schools only educated a small percentage of the population, and the system still suffered from teacher shortages, high dropout rates, and an attendance rate of about 10 percent. Such schools served only cities, towns, and a few larger villages.

Further complicating matters, Amharic was the language of instruction for all schools throughout the country, despite the fact that many of Ethiopia's citizens outside of the Central Plateau did not speak this language. Illiteracy remained common throughout most of the country.

Ethiopia's education system made many advances under the Derg. The country's number of schools more than doubled during the regime's first ten years. Furthermore, the Derg emphasized a curriculum that addressed local and rural needs. As a result, literacy became more widespread, although more than half the population remained illiterate.

In 1993 the country's educational system allowed subjects to be taught in local languages for the first time. In addition, teaching has become geared more toward the culture and needs of a region's particular ethnic group. Recent years have seen a steady increase in school enrollment. According to the Ethiopian government, about 4 million students are enrolled in primary schools. Most Ethiopian students, however, do not go beyond the primary school level, averaging about five years of education. About 900,000 are enrolled in secondary schools. Despite this progress, more than half of Ethiopians over the age of fifteen are illiterate—including 69 percent of adult women.

◉ Women

Ethiopian women do not enjoy many of the legal rights Western women have. Until recently, Ethiopian law stated that the husband was the head of the family and the sole owner of all of a family's property. Women did not have the right to own land, and if a woman's husband died, she often lost the rights to the family's land. But a new law passed by the Ethiopian government has helped to change this situation, and the Ethiopian constitution states that women have the right to own land.

Not all brides in Ethiopia follow traditional **marriage rituals.** Some are permitted to marry a man of their choosing and may even participate in Western-style wedding ceremonies *(above).*

In most cases, parents arrange marriages in Ethiopia—as opposed to the bride and groom choosing one another. A recent law has made it illegal to marry a girl under the age of eighteen, but despite this, many girls are married at age ten or even eight in rural areas. Ethiopia also has no laws protecting women from domestic violence and sexual harassment in the workplace.

Ethiopian women have limited opportunities for employment and education. In some rural areas, where few young people attend school to begin with, attendance by girls is almost nonexistent. Rural women generally perform domestic duties such as cooking, cleaning, caring for children, and helping with farmwork. Ethiopian women living in urban areas are more likely to attend school. Employment opportunities for urban women are generally limited to the service sector, including such jobs as hotel, shop, and restaurant workers, and some factory labor.

CULTURAL LIFE

It would be impossible to strictly define Ethiopian culture, as it is as wide and varied as the nation's many different ethnic groups. Numerous religions and traditions have evolved and mingled in unique ways to create a fascinating and diverse range of lifestyles. Moreover, Ethiopia's rural setting, with its lack of roads and means of communication among regions, has fostered long-standing cultures, many of which have changed little since earlier generations.

◉ Religion

About 40 percent of the people of Ethiopia—most of them Amhara and Tigray—are members of the Ethiopian Orthodox Church, which belongs to the Monophysite (single-nature) branch of Christianity. The Monophysites split from the main body of Christianity in the sixth century A.D. over the question of whether Jesus was human and divine in one nature or in two separate natures. The Ethiopians supported the single-nature theory. For the average Ethiopian Christian, however,

such questions seem distant, and it is the local clergy who play the largest role in daily religious life. Several priests are needed to say the ritual Mass, which is said in the ancient Geez language, and deacons perform secondary functions in the rite.

The Church's practices are quite strict. Members are expected to fast—skip breakfast and eat only vegetables for the rest of the day—165 days a year, including every Wednesday and Friday and throughout Lent and Easter. (Clergy fast 250 days a year.) Ethiopian Christians must attend services each Sunday and on all holy days. These services begin at 6 A.M. and last for three hours, while the Easter service begins on the Friday before Easter and ends at midnight on Easter Sunday. Worshipers are expected to stand throughout the entire service.

Between 40 and 50 percent of Ethiopians are Muslims, who follow Islam, a religion that was developed on the Arabian Peninsula in the seventh century A.D. Islam centers on the teachings of the prophet Muhammad, who claimed to have received the word of God through a series of divine revelations. The revelations were later recorded in the Muslim holy book, the Quran.

Islam is not just a religion but a way of life, revolving around the "five pillars of faith." These include the recitation of the *shahada,* proclaiming faith in God and his prophet Muhammad; praying five times each day (at sunrise, at midday, in midafternoon, at sunset, and at night); almsgiving (assisting the poor); fasting during the holy month of Ramadan; and making a pilgrimage to the holy city of Mecca in Saudi Arabia at least once in a lifetime, if possible.

Most of Ethiopia's Muslims live in the lowland regions in the south and east of the country. The city of Harer, home to dozens of mosques (Muslim places of worship), is the religion's cultural center in Ethiopia. In some regions, religious customs and observance are less formal, mainly because the lifestyle in these areas often makes it difficult to follow Muslim rules. For example, the fasting during Ramadan—which includes not drinking water throughout the day—is often not possible for a poor farmer who must work in a harsh climate.

Traditional beliefs in the power of nature and in a natural life force—often termed animism—are practiced by about 12 percent of Ethiopians. Such beliefs are rarely based on holy books, or text, but are rather traditions passed down over many generations. The different sets of beliefs are as varied as Ethiopia's many different ethnic groups. Even those who support another faith, however, may combine elements of these ancient ideas into their own religious beliefs.

A unique religious minority—the Ethiopian Jews (called Falasha in Amharic)—believes in a mixture of Judaic and traditional African ideas. This sect does not practice the Talmud (traditional Jewish authority) and knows no Hebrew (the traditional language of Jewish religious writings). Falasha scriptures are written in Geez. Although they observe the Jewish feast of Passover, Purim—another Jewish festival—is unknown to them.

In 1984 and 1985, about 8,000 Ethiopian Jews were airlifted to the Jewish state of Israel from Sudan, where the Falasha had fled from Ethiopia's famine and wars. Although they no longer face such dire problems, the Falasha of Israel have at times struggled to adjust to a modern

Ethiopia is one of a handful of countries that still uses the Julian calendar, which is made up of twelve equal months of thirty days each and a thirteenth month of five or six days, depending on the year. The Julian calendar was first adopted in the first century A.D. in Rome. Most countries, including the United States, use the Gregorian calendar, which was created in 1582.

Ethiopian Jews descend from a plane in Israel, having fled Ethiopia's famine and civil wars. However, some Falasha have had trouble adjusting to life in their new country, where their religious authenticity has been questioned.

society. By 1992 nearly all the Falasha had left Ethiopia. Among the few who remain, most live in the Gonder region and in Addis Ababa.

Literature

Most Ethiopian literature was written in either the ancient language of Geez or in Amharic. Much of Ethiopia's ancient literature is religious in nature, and the earliest surviving Ethiopian literary works are Geez translations of Greek religious writings. Through the centuries, Ethiopian literature flourished or stagnated depending on the interest of the rulers of the time.

The return of the Solomonic line in the thirteenth century brought about a revival of writing, and a number of notable works were produced in the following centuries. These include the fourteenth-century *Kebra Negast* (*Glory of the Kings*), a collection of mythical stories centered on Maqueda, the queen of Sheba, and her son, Menelik. The fifteenth century produced an array of religious poetry, as well as a number of works describing the lives of saints, including the life of Saint George, the patron saint of Ethiopia.

By the sixteenth century, Geez was on the wane as a conversational and literary language, although it continues to be used in the Orthodox Church. In turn, more and more literature began to appear in Amharic, the language spoken by many Ethiopians. Most early Amharic writings were translations of Christian religious works. The first Amharic translation of the Bible and chronicles of Ethiopian emperors were produced in the nineteenth century.

In the early decades of his reign, Haile Selassie supported Amharic literature, and many works were written during this period, including histories, plays, biographies, and novels. But in the decades following World War II, literary works began to voice the public's hostility toward

RASTAFARIANS

Interestingly, the *Kebra Negast* is a holy book to the Rastafarians, a religious and political movement founded in the 1920s in the Caribbean island nation of Jamaica by descendants of African slaves. Early Rastafarians believed that all Africans were descendants of the ancient Israelites and that the slavery of black Africans was a punishment from God for disobedience. Rastafarians also considered Emperor Haile Selassie—also known as Ras Tafari—to be a god and the champion of the black race. They believed that the emperor would one day arrange for all people of African descent to be returned to Africa.

Haile Selassie did not believe he was a god. He visited Jamaica in the mid-1960s and was confused by Rastafarians who worshiped him. Nevertheless, some Rastafarians have moved to Ethiopia and set up communities there. Several hundred Rastafarians live in Ethiopia in the early 2000s.

the emperor's increasingly unpopular regime. Censorship was imposed, and many books were banned. After the fall of the monarchy, the Derg also engaged in censorship while promoting works that praised the new government and socialism.

Recent Ethiopian literature often touches on themes such as village life and tensions between Christianity and traditional religion, and between urban and rural life. Among the handful of Ethiopian authors published in English, Berhane Mariam Sahle Selassie is the most widely known. His works include the novels *Shinega's Village: Scenes of Ethiopian Life* (1964); *Warrior King* (1974), a work of historical fiction based on the life of Emperor Tewodros II; and *Firebrands* (1979), a scathing indictment of government corruption.

◉ The Arts

In a country where many people are unable to read, the acting out of religious and historical events has been especially important. Ethiopia's many ethnic groups have handed down their stories and traditions in a variety of ways.

Western-style drama is a fairly new form of art in Ethiopia. The first Western-style play—*Yawrewoch Komediya* (*Comedy of the Animals*), a comedy based on the fables of the seventeenth-century French writer Jean de La Fontaine—was performed for Emperor Menelik II in Amharic. Theater flourished during the early decades of Haile Selassie's reign. Drama classes were part of the curriculum in some schools, and the emperor commissioned a 1,400-seat theater, later named the National Theater, in the 1950s. From this period emerged Ethiopia's best-known playwright and actor, Alem-tsehay Wedajo, who has written plays both in Amharic and English.

The Mengistu regime at first promoted theater by supporting plays that furthered its socialist goals. But as the Derg became unpopular and dramas became more critical of the government, censorship was enforced. As a result, many Ethiopian playwrights and theater companies stopped producing original works and focused their energies on performing Amharic translations of classic plays, such as the works of William Shakespeare and ancient Greek dramas.

Since the fall of the Mengistu regime, Ethiopian theater has experienced a renaissance, with a large number of theater companies opening in Addis Ababa. Many of these groups are producing original works that touch on Ethiopian daily life and politics.

Beautiful Ethiopian songs, written about the land and its people, are accompanied by a variety of instruments, such as the *kerar* (a harplike instrument) and the *masenko* (akin to a violin). The latter has only one string and is played with a bow. The *meleket*, a type of horn, is the most popular wind instrument and is made of wood covered with animal hide. About 3.5 feet (1 m) in length, it resembles a combination of an ancient Greek trumpet and a Latin tuba. Much of Ethiopia's music is related to church traditions. In Ethiopian churches, the only instruments used are *sistrums* (metal rattles) and drums to accompany choirs.

Ethiopia has a long tradition of religious and historical painting. Many beautifully illustrated manuscripts remain from the Middle Ages, and the walls of churches and public buildings are adorned with paintings. These artworks show a strong resemblance to Byzantine and Romanesque styles of painting and mosaics. Modern painting is represented by the works of

Ethiopian religious art is meant to instruct and inspire those who are unable to read the religious texts themselves, much like the artwork found in many European churches.

Afewerk Tekle, who is considered one of the most talented artists in Ethiopia. His stained-glass windows in Africa Hall are alive with color.

Most Ethiopians, especially women, are skilled at making household objects such as the *messob*, a decorated stand from which Ethiopian dishes are customarily served. Girls and women commonly weave carpets, and beautiful earthenware pots are also made by hand. Many Ethiopian men are skilled goldsmiths, several of whom are famous for their gold and silver objects used in church services.

● Food and Clothing

The staple foods of the country are maize (corn), barley, wheat, and teff (a grain native to Ethiopia). Although wheat is grown, flour is commonly produced from teff, which is made into unleavened bread, such as *injera*, or into noodles. A typical dish in Ethiopian cuisine is *wat*,

INJERA

Injera is the staple food for many Ethiopians. It is served with most meals, where it is accompanied by meat, vegetables, and often a spicy sauce. Injera is usually made with flour from the Ethiopian grain teff, which can be difficult to find in the West, so a self-rising flour has been substituted in this recipe.

3 c. warm water   **3 tbsp. club soda**
2½ c. self-rising flour   **½ tsp. vegetable oil**

1. Pour warm water into a blender or food processor. Add the flour, cover, and blend on low for 10 seconds. Turn blender on high and mix for 30 seconds, until smooth.
2. Pour the batter into a mixing bowl and add the club soda. Mix with a spoon. The batter should have a consistency of heavy cream.
3. Bring a small skillet to medium heat. Spread a little oil over the pan with a pastry brush or paper towel. Use a ladle to pour ½ c. of the batter to one side of the pan. Quickly tilt the pan to spread the batter evenly over the bottom.
4. Small bubbles will soon appear on the surface, and the edges of the pancake will curl away from the pan. After 1 minute, use a spatula to remove the injera. Place it on a flour sack or kitchen towel to cool. The finished injera should be white and easy to bend. Repeat the process until the batter is used up.
5. Fold each injera in quarters and stack on a plate to serve. Serves 6 to 8 people.

which is prepared with meat, chicken, and a hot pepper sauce and eaten with injera. At high altitudes, where sheep are raised, lamb is eaten. Goat and camel meat are popular at lower elevations. Popular beverages include coffee, tea, *tej* (a sweet wine made from honey), and barley-based beer, called *tella.*

Ethiopian clothing styles are as diverse as the country's many different ethnic groups and regions. In urban areas such as Addis Ababa, many citizens wear Western-style clothing. Ethiopians living in the highlands often wear the *shamma,* a traditional robe of white cotton with brightly colored borders. Pastoral peoples of the Lowlands often wear leather clothes and bead or shell jewelry. The people of the Harer region wear colorful garments and thin veils.

● Festivals

Festivals and holidays, both religious and secular, provide Ethiopians with important opportunities for celebration, recreation, and socializing. Many of Ethiopia's holidays involve religious festivals tied to the Ethiopian Orthodox Church, although the nation's Muslims and other religious groups celebrate their own holidays. Muslims observe the holy month of Ramadan and the birth of the prophet Muhammad, while animists often celebrate the change of season, harvests, and important life events, such as births and weddings.

Among Christian holidays, Timkat, the Feast of the Epiphany, is the most important. Timkat celebrates the baptism of Jesus and falls

The lighting of large bonfires commences the Maskal festival each September. Priests dress in their finest attire and everyone sings and dances.

on January 19. Celebrations often last three days and include parades, processions, all-night prayer vigils, feasts, and the exchanging of gifts.

Christmas, or Ganna, the day celebrating the birth of Jesus, is also an important holiday among Ethiopian Christians. The day (January 4) begins with Mass, sometimes beginning as early as 3 A.M. and lasting for several hours. After a special celebratory meal, many Christians participate in a game called *ganna*, which is similar to the sport field hockey.

The Ethiopian New Year is celebrated at the end of the rainy season, on September 11. Called Enkutatash, which means "gift of jewels," the day commemorates the queen of Sheba's return from the court of King Solomon, at which time she was given many precious jewels. The holiday is often celebrated by the lighting of bonfires on New Year's Eve.

Two weeks following Enkutatash, Ethiopians celebrate Maskal, which honors both the finding of the true cross on which Jesus is said to have been crucified. The cross is said to have been awarded to Ethiopia's kings for their service in protecting the country's Christian minority from harm about 1,600 years ago. Maskal celebrations include dancing, feasts, parades, and the setting of bonfires.

Secular holidays include Labor Day (May 1), Ethiopian Patriots Victory Day (May 5), and the anniversary of the Battle of Adwa (March 2). The latter holiday celebrates Menelik II's triumph over the Italians at Adwa, the first major victory of African forces over European forces and the event that secured European recognition of Ethiopian independence.

To learn more about Ethiopian cultural life, visit www.vgsbooks.com. There you'll find links to information on Ethiopia's many traditions, including music, religious and contemporary art, food and recipes, holidays and festivals, sports, and more.

Sports and Recreation

Among sports, soccer is the most popular game in Ethiopia. Both children and adults play in leagues and informal matches, and a national tournament is held each year in Addis Ababa. Soccer is also the most popular spectator sport in Ethiopia.

Long-distance running is also important, and the country's high-altitude regions are a perfect training ground for world-class runners. Several Ethiopians have won medals in Olympic competition. The most famous Ethiopian runner is Abebe Bikila, a former member of Haile Selassie's Imperial Guard who became a national hero by winning the gold medal in the marathon competition at the 1960 Olympic Games in Rome, Italy. Bikila won the event again in the 1964 Olympics in Tokyo, Japan.

Ethiopian long-distance runners Derartu Tulu (*right*) and Berhane Adere (*left*) finish the 10,000-meter race in the eighth International Association of Athletics Federations (IAAF) World Championships in Athletics in Edmonton, Canada.

Ethiopians also enjoy a number of sports unique to their country. These include *kwosso,* a fast, rough-and-tumble game in which two teams play keep-away with a goatskin ball. Kwosso is popular among the Afar people of Ethiopia's northeast. Another rough game, *feres gugs,* is played on horseback and involves opposing players striking one another with wooden sticks and dodging these attacks.

Among less physical forms of competition, a board game called *gabata* is the most popular. The game uses a wooden board and seeds for pieces. Like chess, gabata has a complex set of rules involving the movement and capture of the pieces.

Ethiopians also pass their free time telling and listening to folktales, singing, and dancing. Popular children's games include *debebekosh,* a kind of hide-and-seek game, and *kelelebosh,* a version of jacks.

THE ECONOMY

Ethiopia is one of the world's poorest countries. The UN Development Program has ranked Ethiopia at 168 out of 173 countries in its human development index, which is based on a combination of statistics—income, literacy, and life expectancy. Most Ethiopians are subsistence farmers who are dangerously vulnerable to drought and famine. In addition, the government's social programs, including health and education, depend heavily on foreign aid donations.

Yet, despite its challenges, Ethiopia has tremendous potential for growth. Half of the country's fertile regions are unused and could be cultivated, and few of its mineral resources have been exploited. In addition, its many rivers carry great potential for hydroelectric power generation. Ethiopia's greatest challenge in reaching its potential is the need to create infrastructure that can facilitate commerce and development.

Since the days of the ancient Aksumite kingdom, Ethiopia has engaged in trade with other regions, such as Arabia and Egypt, through which Ethiopian gold, ivory, and animal skins were exchanged for

exotic items such as silk and velvet. By the nineteenth century, Ethiopian coffee had become a major cash crop, but aside from a small class of coffee producers, Ethiopia remained a country made up mostly of subsistence farmers with little industrialization or manufacturing. Most farmers cultivated small plots of land, herded cattle, or both. Many nomadic peoples raised livestock, moving from one area to the next as the seasons changed.

In the decades following World War II, the government of Haile Selassie focused on developing more industry. As a result, ambitious plans were laid out to improve Ethiopia's infrastructure, including building more roads, highways, and telephone lines to link isolated regions, and the expansion of the electricity grid. In addition, the government sought to train a new class of workers to work in skilled manufacturing jobs. While some progress was made in each of these programs, the government lacked the financial resources and trained personnel to meet its ambitious goals, and the country remained primarily a subsistence economy.

Not all farming in Ethiopia is done by subsistence farmers. This farmer is **cultivating herbs** to be used in traditional medicine at the Ethiopian Health and Nutrition Research Institute. The institute stores more than 800 plants commonly used by traditional healers.

The Mengistu regime imposed radical changes to the Ethiopian economy, including the nationalization of all banks and industries, and the collectivization of farmland. While the country did see improvement in harvests and living conditions during years of good weather, the droughts of the mid-1980s forced the government to divert its development resources toward famine relief. In addition, the Mengistu regime's large military expenses—which accounted for up to half the government's expenses during the early 1980s—placed a strain on the Ethiopian economy.

Following the fall of Mengistu, the new Ethiopian government has worked toward reforming and modernizing the economy. This process has included privatizing many businesses and reducing defense spending by cutting the size of the armed forces. Some progress was made toward improving the Ethiopian standard of living in the early 1990s. But the 1998–2000 war with Eritrea—which cost the government an estimated $2.9 billion—coupled with a prolonged drought from 1999 through 2002, have created more setbacks.

Agriculture

Farming is the major occupation of about four-fifths of all Ethiopians. Agriculture contributes about 52 percent of Ethiopia's gross domestic product (GDP), the total value of goods and services produced by a nation in a year. As an agricultural nation, Ethiopia has tremendous potential. Only about 12 percent of the country's lands are under cultivation, and much of the uncultivated lands contain fertile soils and good rainfall. In 2003 the Ethiopian government unveiled a program that would encourage farmers to move from drought-stricken regions to these more fertile areas.

Meanwhile, Ethiopia's existing farmland often does not yield its full potential, due to soil erosion and the lack of irrigation, modern equipment, and fertilizer. Only about 4 percent of Ethiopia's lands are irrigated. Modern equipment is not readily available to small-scale farmers, who use horses, oxen, and basic agricultural tools for plowing and harvesting. Fertilizer is often unaffordable for most farmers.

In recent years, Ethiopia's farmers have struggled with a difficult cycle. During good harvest years, an overabundance of grain drives down prices. Farmers are unable to reinvest their earnings into better seeds, fertilizer, and irrigation systems that could improve their farmlands in the future.

Grains, such as teff, wheat, and barley, are grown widely in the highlands from 5,000 to 11,500 feet (1,524 to 3,505 m) above sea level. Secondary cereal grains, such as maize, sorghum, and millet, are produced in the western, southwestern, and eastern parts of the country. These regions have the warmer climate and lower altitudes that such crops need. Sorghum and millet also resist drought conditions, growing well in areas that do not receive much rainfall.

Pulses (the adult seeds of various crops) such as chickpeas, lentils, and haricot beans grow well at all altitudes

KEEPING COOL

Both honey and beeswax are major cash crops in Ethiopia. The country is the world's tenth largest producer of honey, and Ethiopians themselves use it to brew tej. Meanwhile, honey is also important for its health benefits. It is used in Ethiopian hospitals to treat high fevers, burning skin, ulcers, colds, coughs, and diseases of the mouth. Honey is even used in cosmetics. Beeswax is also a vital cash crop, competing even with coffee as one of Ethiopia's top export commodities.

Honey production hives at the Biofarm in Addis Ababa. To find links where you can learn more about beekeeping and other natural health farming methods in Ethiopia, visit www.vgsbooks.com.

One of Ethiopia's most lucrative crops is khat, the leaves of a large shrub known as the *Catha edulis*. Many people throughout the Horn of Africa region and the Middle East chew khat leaves for their narcotic effect. The drug produces a mild sense of euphoria and dulls the feeling of hunger but is believed to be addictive. Regardless, khat is Ethiopia's second biggest export crop, after coffee, with the country earning about $60 million from khat cultivation each year. While discouraging its use, the Ethiopian government has no clear policy on the cultivation and sale of the drug, which is illegal in the United States and Canada.

but are most often found in the northern and central highlands. Oilseed production is stimulated by an unlikely source—the Ethiopian Orthodox Church. Its restrictions against the use of animal fats have encouraged the cultivation of vegetable oilseeds, such as linseed, Niger seed, and sesame seed.

Coffee is a cash crop and the country's largest export commodity, accounting for more than two-thirds of the nation's export trade. But falling coffee prices on the world market have devastated the Ethiopian economy in recent years. In 1997–1998, Ethiopia earned $453 million from coffee exports, but by the early 2000s, earnings had dropped to $170 million each year. Khat, a mild narcotic leaf that is illegal in some countries, is also exported widely from Ethiopia throughout the Middle East and East Africa. Because of Ethiopia's location within the tropics, citrus fruits, bananas, and vegetables—such as cabbages, onions, peppers, and lettuce—also thrive.

Livestock and animal products—primarily hides and skins—are Ethiopia's second most important export commodity. Ethiopia holds the largest total livestock herds in Africa. In the early 2000s, an estimated 68 million sheep, goats, and cattle grazed on Ethiopia's pastureland, along with about 2.8 million horses and 1 million camels. Years of drought have decreased these numbers, but by how much is unknown.

Industry and Trade

Industry, which includes both mining and manufacturing, makes up about 11 percent of Ethiopia's GDP and employs about 8 percent of the country's workforce. Most of Ethiopia's manufactured products are made for domestic use. They include food, textiles, and beverages. Other manufactured products include tobacco, leather shoes, printing, and items made of wood, steel, and cement. Among export commodities, vegetables, fruit, livestock, and coffee are major items, although

Miners fashion bricks from salt in the Danakil Depression. For centuries Ethiopians have used salt to barter for essential items at the marketplace.

Ethiopia often lags behind its competing neighbor countries, such as Kenya, in the marketing and packaging of its goods.

In recent years, Ethiopia has begun to make use of its significant proven reserves of valuable minerals, including gold, coal, potassium, and iron ore. The Lega Dembi Gold Mine in southern Ethiopia is Ethiopia's largest, producing 660 pounds (300 kilograms) each year. Meanwhile, the Danakil Depression in the northeast is renowned for its salt and potash deposits. Ethiopia has underground petroleum reserves, but the government has not yet invested in exploration or drilling.

Ethiopia's main trading partners are the United States, Saudi Arabia, Western Europe, and Japan. The country carries a trade deficit, meaning it imports significantly more goods than it exports.

◉ Services and Tourism

About 12 percent of Ethiopians work in the service sector, which includes government, tourism-related services, and retail. Services make up about 37 percent of Ethiopia's GDP. Ethiopia does not have a thriving tourism industry, and for many years, the country closed its doors to tourists. The country's isolation was most complete during the Mengistu regime, when internal strife was at its height. In recent years,

however, the Ethiopian Tourist Commission has opened up opportunities for foreign visitors to explore the many historical, cultural, and natural phenomena within Ethiopia. Some 136,000 foreigners visited Ethiopia in 2000, adding about $24 million in revenue to the country. Ethiopia's tourism industry, however, suffered a downturn in the wake of the September 11, 2001, attacks on the United States. The terrorist attacks caused many people to forgo air travel, causing a worldwide tourism slump. Accompanied by official guides of the commission, foreigners can travel to the castles of Gonder or visit the rock churches of Lalibela or enjoy beautiful views of Blue Nile Gorge and Blue Nile Falls.

In 2002 the Ethiopian government commissioned the building of a giant dam on the Tekeze River in northern Ethiopia. When completed, the $224-million facility will provide not only 300 megawatts of electricity, but will also help with irrigation of the region's croplands.

Ethiopia has set aside several areas as parkland. The Bale Mountains

Tourists on safari scan the plains for wildlife in Mago National Park in southwestern Ethiopia.

National Park, in south-central Ethiopia, includes moorlands, high peaks, alpine lakes, and lava flows. The park is the largest alpine area under protection in Africa. Other parks include Mago National Park and Omo National Park, which lie along the Omo River in the southwest, Gambella National Park near the Sudanese border, and Yangudi Rassa National Park in the east, north of Dire Dawa.

Energy

Wood and charcoal are the most common fuels for the average Ethiopian. On a large scale, however, the most extensive source of energy is hydroelectric power, which is estimated to provide about 1.7 billion kilowatt-hours a year. Ethiopia's rivers have the potential to meet all of Ethiopia's energy needs. The country's first hydropower plants were built on the Awash River between 1960 and 1970. In 1974 Ethiopia's largest complex was put into operation on a tributary of the Blue Nile. New dams are being planned, and one project has already begun on the Tekeze River. But Ethiopia's plans to dam the Nile River have strained its relations with its neighbors downriver. Both Sudan and Egypt have expressed concern over Ethiopia's exploitation of the Nile, fearing that Ethiopian dams may restrict or diminish the flow of the Nile's waters in their countries.

Ethiopia has recently begun construction of its first geothermal energy plant—located in the Great Rift Valley— which will use the heat of the earth's interior to provide energy. The country's location within the tropics also provides the nation with the potential for solar energy. Many scientists feel that solar energy—provided by individual solar panels installed in homes, as opposed to other forms requiring a huge electrical grid—is the best answer for providing electricity to predominantly rural countries like Ethiopia.

Transportation and Communications

Lack of good transportation and communication infrastructure is a key obstacle to Ethiopia's economic development. Because of the country's rugged terrain and seasonal weather problems, highways are few and fail to meet the economic and social needs of the people. Most villages, mineral-rich regions, and agricultural lands are inaccessible. Pack animals and occasionally airplanes provide transportation to these isolated regions. In recent years, the Ethiopian government has made the building and maintenance of roads a high priority, devoting 20 percent of the federal budget to this purpose.

Ethiopia's only railroad line—between Addis Ababa and neighboring Djibouti—moves import and export commodities. Water transportation is used in some parts of the country, particularly around Lake Tana and the Great Rift Valley lakes and on rivers in the south. Ethiopian Airlines is one of the busiest and most successful African airlines, handling transportation from Addis Ababa to major cities within Ethiopia and to parts of Africa, Europe, and Asia.

Ethiopia has four daily newspapers, with a total circulation of about 89,000. Most Ethiopians do not have access to electronic

Though travel within Ethiopia is often difficult because of poorly maintained roads, air travel is becoming more widespread as companies such as **Ethiopian Airlines** offer more service to remote areas.

communications, such as telephones, televisions, and the Internet. In a nation of 70.7 million people, only about 367,000 televisions and 310,000 telephones are in use. The country has about 75,000 personal computers and 25,000 Internet users. About 27,500 Ethiopians subscribe to mobile phone services.

 Visit www.vgsbooks.com for links to discover more about Ethiopia's economy. Convert U.S. dollars into Ethiopian birr, learn about farming regions and techniques, and more.

The Future

Although poverty, famine, and war have brought hardship to many Ethiopians in recent decades, the country still holds the potential for a bright future. With agricultural, mineral, hydroelectric, and geothermal resources yet to be tapped, Ethiopia possesses tremendous opportunities for growth in the coming decades. The EPRDF government continues to work—often in consultation with international aid organizations—toward eliminating the country's recurring cycle of famine and improving the standard of living for Ethiopia's citizens.

Yet conflicts—both internal and external—continue to threaten Ethiopia's development. The ongoing border dispute with Eritrea threatens to erupt into another costly war. Final demarcation of the Ethiopian-Eritrean border, originally scheduled for October 2003, has been delayed due to disagreements over the exact placement of the boundary. Meanwhile, within Ethiopia, the OLF continues to engage in sporadic guerrilla attacks on government facilities. Other ethnic groups also complain that their interests are not being adequately represented in the Tigray- and Amhara-dominated government.

As a nation with beautiful landscapes, a unique and rich history, and a stunning variety of peoples and cultures, Ethiopia continues to fascinate. If the country's challenges can be met and its development continues, Ethiopia may well enjoy a prosperous future.

CA. 2000-1000 B.C.	Immigrants from Sheba, a kingdom in Arabia, move into Ethiopia and mingle with the native peoples of the region.
CA. 1000-900 B.C.	According to legend, Maqueda, queen of Sheba, visits the court of King Solomon of Israel. Maqueda and Solomon conceive a son, Menelik I.
CA. A.D. 100	The Aksumite kingdom is established with its capital at Aksum, in northern Ethiopia.
CA. 300	King Ezana of Aksum converts to Christianity. The religion soon takes hold throughout the kingdom.
CA. 300-600	The Aksumite kingdom grows to cover most of modern-day Eritrea and Tigray and Welo provinces. Aksum's port at Adulis, on the Red Sea, is a hub of world trade.
CA. 600-900	Muslim invasions weaken Aksumite rule. The kingdom loses all of its lands by the tenth century.
CA. 1130s	The Zagwe, a Cushitic people from the Lasta Mountains, establish a Christian dynasty in Roha (modern-day Lalibela).
1270	Yekuno Amlaq, a prince who claims descent from the Solomonic line, deposes the Zagwe ruler and reestablishes the Solomonic dynasty.
1529	A Muslim invasion, led by Ahmad ibn Ibrahim al-Ghazi, penetrates into the heart of Ethiopia.
1543	Ethiopian ruler Gelawdewos, with the help of Portuguese weapons and soldiers, defeats al-Ghazi in a climactic battle.
CA. 1769-1855	Political turmoil weakens the Solomonic dynasty, leading to the Era of the Princes, during which the weak emperors hold little power over local rulers.
1855	Tewodros II is crowned emperor. He goes on to unify much of the country under his rule, thus ending the Era of the Princes.
1872	The ruler of Tigray is crowned Emperor John IV.
1882	John IV drives out a force of Italians that had invaded northern Ethiopia.
1889	John IV dies in battle fighting Mahdists from Sudan. Menelik II succeeds him as emperor.
1896	Ethiopian armies, under the command of Menelik II, score a decisive victory over Italian forces at the Battle of Adwa, assuring Ethiopia's independence from European rule.

1913 Menelik II dies. His grandson Lij Ayasu succeeds him.

1916 Christian nobles depose Lij Ayasu. They replace him with Menelik II's daughter, Zauditu. Ras Tafari is named regent and heir to the throne.

1923 Ethiopia joins the League of Nations.

1930 Upon the death of Zauditu, Ras Tafari becomes Emperor Haile Selassie I.

1935 Italian troops invade and occupy Ethiopia. Haile Selassie flees the country.

1941 Ethiopian and British forces drive Italian forces out of Ethiopia. Haile Selassie returns to power.

1952 A UN resolution declares Eritrea to be a part of Ethiopia.

1961 The Eritrean Liberation Front (ELF) is formed, and the group begins to wage guerrilla war against the Ethiopian government.

1973 Famine strikes northern and eastern Ethiopia.

1974 A group of military officers deposes Haile Selassie on September 12. The officers establish the Derg, a committee that will rule the country and begin to transform Ethiopia into a socialist state.

1976 Mengistu Haile-Mariam emerges as the dictator of Ethiopia.

1984 After a long drought, massive famine spreads throughout much of the country. Due to government denials of the situation, tens of thousands of Ethiopians die before international aid is delivered.

1991 Rebel attacks on the capital cause Mengistu to flee the country on May 21. A new provisional government is declared, with Meles Zenawi as leader.

1993 Eritrea declares its independence on May 24.

1995 Elections are held and a new government is formed with Meles Zenawi as prime minister.

1998 A border dispute between Ethiopia and Eritrea leads to war between the two countries.

2000 A peace agreement between Ethiopia and Eritrea is signed in June, but tensions remain high.

2004 More than four straight years of drought leave about 7 million Ethiopians in danger of starvation. Plans for the final demarcation of the Ethiopia-Eritrean border remain unresolved.

COUNTRY NAME Federal Democratic Republic of Ethiopia

AREA 426,373 square miles (1,104,301 sq. km)

MAIN LANDFORMS Great Rift Valley, Central Plateau, Danakil Depression, Lowlands, Simyen Mountains, Choke Mountains, Ahmar Mountains, Mendebo Mountains

HIGHEST POINT Ras Dashen, 15,158 feet (4,620 m) above sea level

LOWEST POINT Danakil Depression, 300 feet (91 m) below sea level

MAJOR RIVERS Akobo, Awash, Baro, Blue Nile (Abbai), Shabeelle, Tekeze

ANIMALS antelope, baboons, civet cats, crocodiles, cuckoos, eagles, elephants, Ethiopian wolves, flamingos, flycatchers, giraffes, hawks, hippopotamuses, hyenas, leopards, lions, rhinoceroses, walia ibex, weaverbirds, zebras

CAPITAL CITY Addis Ababa

OTHER MAJOR CITIES Aksum, Debre Markos, Dese, Dire Dawa, Gonder, Harer,

OFFICIAL LANGUAGE Amharic

MONETARY UNIT Birr. 100 cents = 1 birr.

ETHIOPIAN CURRENCY

The birr is the currency of the Federal Democratic Republic of Ethiopia. Also referred to as the dux, or the dollar, birr notes are printed in denominations of 1, 5, 10, 50, and 100. The Ethiopian government began circulating new bills in 1998 to replace the old notes of the Derg. The new birr notes are inscribed in both Amharic and English and come in brown, gray, blue, orange, and green. They feature agricultural scenes, animals, plants, and landmarks. The Ethiopian government also mints 50, 25, 10, 5, and 1 cent (sometimes called centimes) pieces.

The Federal Democratic Republic of Ethiopia adopted its current flag in 1996. It consists of three horizontal stripes of green, yellow, and red. A light-blue emblem in the center features a five-pointed star. The green stripe symbolizes the fertility of Ethiopia's lands, the yellow stripe symbolizes the country's religious freedom, and the red stands for the blood sacrificed to maintain Ethiopia's freedom. The five-pointed star is a symbol of the unity of the country's many different regions and ethnic groups.

The Ethiopian national anthem was adopted in 1992, following the fall of the Derg. The lyrics, written in Amharic by Dereje Melaku Mengesha, spotlight Ethiopians' proud heritage of courage and hard work. The anthem's music was composed by Solomon Lulu Mitiku.

Whedefit Gesgeshi Woude Henate Ethiopia
(March Forward, Dear Mother Ethiopia)
Respect for citizenship is strong in our Ethiopia;
National pride is seen, shining from one side to another.
For peace, for justice, for the freedom of peoples,
In equality and in love we stand united.
Firm of foundation, we do not dismiss humanness;
We are peoples who live through work.
Wonderful is the stage of tradition, mistress of proud heritage,
Mother of natural virtue, mother of a valorous people.
We shall protect you, we have a duty;
Our Ethiopia, live! And let us be proud of you!

For a link where you can listen to Ethiopia's national anthem, "Whedefit Gesgeshi Woude Henate Ethiopia" (March Forward, Dear Mother Ethiopia), go to www.vgsbooks.com.

ABEBE BIKILA (1932–1973) Born in the town of Jato in Shewa Province, Abebe is a national hero and the first in a long line of world-class long-distance runners. A talented athlete, Abebe became a national champion marathoner and represented Ethiopia at the 1960 Olympic Games in Rome, Italy. There he set a new world record, running the 26.2-mile (42.2 km) race barefoot. In the 1964 Olympic Games in Tokyo, Abebe again won the gold medal and set a world record, running just six weeks after an operation to remove his appendix.

AFEWERK TEKLE (b. 1932) Ethiopia's most famous and decorated artist was born in Shewa Province. He has worked in a wide variety of mediums, creating drawings, paintings, murals, mosaics, stained-glass windows, and sculptures. His works have appeared on everything from postage stamps to flags and ceremonial dresses.

ASTER AWEKE (b. 1960) One of Ethiopia's best-known singers, Aster was born in Gonder. The daughter of a government official, she began singing with local groups while in her teens and produced a number of recordings. She soon became a household name throughout Ethiopia. Fleeing the civil unrest in her native country, Aster moved to the United States in the early 1980s. Since then she has made several albums, including *Aster* (1989), *Kabu* (1991), *Ebo* (1993), and *Live in London* (1997). She remains a highly popular figure in Ethiopia.

HAILE GEBRSELASSIE (b. 1973) One of Ethiopia's top runners, Gebrselassie was born in Arsi. As a boy, he ran more than 6 miles (10 km) to school and then back home each day. As an adult, he ran with his left arm at his side as a result of the many years spent running with his books tucked under his arm. A world record holder in the 10,000-meter race, he won gold medals in the 1996 Olympic Games in Atlanta, Georgia, as well as at the 2000 games in Sydney, Australia.

HAILE SELASSIE I (1892–1975) Born Tafari Makonnen near Harer, Selassie was the governor of the Harerge Province under his uncle, Menelik II. Serving as regent to Empress Zauditu, he took the name Ras Tafari and fostered progressive reforms that included the building of modern schools and hospitals. He became emperor upon Zauditu's death in 1930, assuming the title Haile Selassie I. Haile Selassie attempted to modernize the country and held a tight grip on power. His rule became increasingly unpopular, and he was deposed in 1974. Months later, he was murdered under mysterious circumstances.

JOHN IV (1831–1889) John IV ruled as emperor for seventeen years. During his reign, he faced many challenges, both from within the empire and from outside forces. While Sahle Mariam (later Menelik II) contested John's right to rule and Ethiopian Muslims protested his attempts to impose the Orthodox Church on them, John successfully fought off attacks by Italian and Egyptian invaders. In the late 1880s, he faced an invasion of Mahdists from Sudan and was killed in battle in 1889.

MELES ZENAWI (b. 1956) Ethiopia's leader since 1991 was born in Adwa. He studied medicine at Addis Ababa University in the early 1970s before becoming a member of the Tigrayan People's Liberation Front (TPLF). With the TPLF and later with the EPRDF, he fought against the Mengistu regime. After Mengistu fled the country in 1991, the Ethiopian provisional government named Meles president. He was elected prime minister in 1995. His government has worked with international aid donors to help modernize the country and bring an end to Ethiopia's cycle of recurring famine.

MENELIK II (1844–1913) Born Sahle Mariam near modern-day Addis Ababa, Menelik II was one of Ethiopia's greatest emperors. He succeeded Emperor John IV in 1889 and became the first African leader to defeat a major European power when his army won a decisive victory over Italian forces at the Battle of Adwa in 1896. The triumph assured Ethiopia's independence and allowed Menelik II to expand his territories and to begin modernizing the country, including building Ethiopia's first railway and founding the country's first modern schools and hospitals.

MENGISTU HAILE-MARIAM (b. 1935) Born in Kefa Province, Mengistu ruled Ethiopia from the mid-1970s to 1991. As an army officer, he played a key role in the overthrow of Emperor Haile Selassie and also ordered the execution of members of the old regime. Mengistu and the Derg sought to make Ethiopia a socialist state by nationalizing industries and collectivizing agriculture. These policies became highly unpopular and, combined with ethnic unrest in Eritrea and the Ogaden, led to civil war throughout much of the country. Facing military defeat, Mengistu fled Ethiopia in 1991 to live in exile in Zimbabwe.

DERARTU TULU (b. 1972) A native of Arsi Province and a member of Ethiopia's Oromo ethnic group, she is the first black African woman to win an Olympic medal. At the 1992 Olympic Games in Barcelona, Spain, Tulu won the gold in a dramatic 10,000-meter race. During the 2000 games in Sydney, Australia, she repeated the feat, becoming the first woman to win two gold medals in Olympic long-distance races.

ZAUDITU (1876–1930) The daughter of Emperor Menelik II, Zauditu ruled as empress of Ethiopia from 1916 until her death in 1930. Because Ethiopian custom discouraged female rulers, a regent, Ras Tafari (the future Haile Selassie I), was appointed to her to assist in ruling the country. Although Ras Tafari controlled much of the day-to-day workings of government, Zauditu held ultimate authority over the country. While the empress occasionally resisted the progressive reforms that her cousin promoted—such as hiring foreign advisers to help modernize the government—Zauditu's rule was characterized by prosperity in the coffee trade and an improvement in Ethiopia's standing on the world stage.

Sights to See

ADDIS ABABA Ethiopia's bustling capital is the country's largest city and home to many attractions. Africa Hall, where the UN Economic Commission for Africa meets, features beautiful stained-glass windows designed by Ethiopian artist Afewerk Tekle. The National Museum features exhibits from several periods of Ethiopian history. The museum holds Lucy, a female fossil skeleton believed to be more than three million years old. The country's many different ethnic groups meet and interact at the Merkato, the largest open-air market in eastern Africa.

AKSUM Located in northern Ethiopia, the seat of the ancient Aksumite kingdom is home to numerous artifacts, including a collection of huge granite stelae, tombs of the ancient kings. The tallest of these carved pillars stands 75 feet (23 m) tall. According to legend, the Ark of the Covenant—an artifact described in the Bible that is said to hold the Ten Commandments—is on the grounds of Saint Mary of Zion Church, but the ark's exact resting place remains a mystery.

GONDER Nestled in the foothills of the Simyen Mountains, Ethiopia's capital from the 1600s until the 1800s is home to many beautiful castles, palaces, and churches. The castles rest within a walled area known as the Imperial City. The most famous structure is Fasilides' Castle, a massive square building erected in the seventeenth century. Subsequent monarchs built their own palaces or castles, each with its own distinctive style.

HARER Located in eastern Ethiopia's Muslim heartland, Harer has been a crossroads of commerce and culture for centuries. The walled city is home to a diverse mix of peoples and religions, including Muslims, Orthodox Christians, and Catholics. Among the city's many attractions is the Magala Guddo, a vibrant and colorful open-air market in the heart of the city.

LALIBELA The former Ethiopian capital is one of the country's most popular tourist attractions, as thousands of visitors from around the world come to visit and worship in the city's eleven rock-hewn churches. The buildings are impressive both for their intricate exterior carvings as well as for their colorful interior murals. Attending the services themselves is like taking a journey back in time, as elaborately dressed priests hold Mass using ancient artifacts and read scripture from antique Bibles written in the traditional language of Geez.

OMO NATIONAL PARK Located along the Omo River in southwestern Ethiopia, this is Ethiopia's largest national park, covering 1,332 square miles (3,450 sq. km). Omo's uninhabited wilderness is home to zebras, oryx, elephants, giraffes, lions, leopards, cheetahs, and many more exotic animals. Several prehistoric fossils have also been found on the site. Some may date back to three million years ago or earlier.

collectivization: a political and economic process through which land or property is taken from individual owners and handed over to a group, or collective, often the state

demarcation: to mark or separate, such as a border between two nations

drought: a period, usually several months or even years, when a region receives little or no precipitation. Droughts can have a devastating effect on farming and lead to famine and disease

dynasty: a family that passes its ruling power from one generation to another

famine: an extreme scarcity of food

gross domestic product (GDP): a measure of the total value of goods and services produced within a country in a certain amount of time (usually one year). A similar measurement is gross national product (GNP). GDP and GNP are often measured in terms of purchasing power parity (PPP). PPP converts values to international dollars, making it possible to compare how much similar goods and services cost to the residents of different countries.

guerrilla war: war characterized by intermittent hit-and-run attacks, as opposed to large battles between armies

infrastructure: the system of public works of a country, including roads, highways, railways, sewers, and telephone lines

League of Nations: an association of nations created after World War I (1914–1918) to help prevent war between countries. Ethiopia was one of the founding members of the League of Nations.

nationalize: to change ownership or control of a business or industry from private to public

pastoralist: a person who raises livestock for a living

socialism: a political and economic theory based on the idea of social rather than individual control of goods and production. In a socialist system, the government owns and controls most businesses and industries.

subsistence farming: a type of farming, prevalent in Ethiopia, in which all of the food grown is needed to feed one's family with little or none left over for commercial sale

tableland: a broad, level, and elevated area of land

teff: a grain native to Ethiopia

Selected Bibliography

BBC (British Broadcasting Corporation) *News Online.* 2003.
<http://news.bbc.co.uk/2/hi/africa/default.stm> (January 9, 2004)
The BBC's Africa section is a helpful resource for news on Ethiopia and other Africa nations.

Central Intelligence Agency (CIA). 2003.
<http://www.odci.gov/cia/publications/factbook/geos/et.html> (January 9, 2004)
The "World Factbook" section of the CIA's website contains basic information on Ethiopia's geography, people, economy, government, communications, transportation, military, and transnational issues.

The Economist. 2003.
<http://www.economist.com> (January 9, 2004)
Both the website and print edition of this British magazine provide up-to-date coverage of Ethiopian news.

Europa Regional Surveys: North Africa 2003. London: Europa Publications Limited, 2003.
This annual publication includes statistics on everything from agriculture and tourism to education and population density. It also contains a detailed account of Ethiopia's recent history and current events, government, military, economy, social welfare, education, and a list of public holidays. Another survey explains details of the Ethiopian government's structure, function, and legal system.

Marcus, Harold G. *A History of Ethiopia.* Berkeley: University of California Press, 1994.
Written by a noted professor of African studies, this book covers in detail the history of Ethiopia from its earliest history to the early 1990s.

Munro-Hay, Stuart. *Ethiopia: The Unknown Land: A Cultural and Historical Guide.* New York: I. B. Tauris Publishers, 2002.
This book, written by a well-known Ethiopian scholar, is a guide to Ethiopia's history, peoples, geography, art, and architecture.

Ofcansky, Thomas P., and LaVerle Berry, eds. *Ethiopia: A Country Study.* Washington, D.C.: Library of Congress, Federal Research Division, 1993.
This volume from the Library of Congress's Area Handbook Series gives detailed information and analysis on Ethiopia's history, society, social welfare, health-care system, education system, environment, economy, government, foreign relations, and national security.

Population Reference Bureau. 2003.
<http://www.prb.org> (January 9, 2004)
The annual statistics on this site provide a wealth of data on Ethiopia's population, birth and death rates, fertility rate, infant mortality rate, and other useful demographic information.

United Nations Integrated Regional Information Networks News.
United Nations Office for the Coordination of Humanitarian Affairs.
Nairobi, Kenya. 2003.
<http://www.irinnews.org> **(January 9, 2004)**
This news service, developed by the UN Office for the Coordination of Humanitarian Affairs, provides up-to-date news stories about humanitarian efforts in developing countries in South Asia and Africa, including Ethiopia.

Ashabranner, Brent K., ed. *The Lion's Whiskers and Other Ethiopian Tales.* **Rev. ed. North Haven, CT: Linnet Books, 1997.**
This illustrated book provides a window onto Ethiopian culture. It contains sixteen Ethiopian folktales, taken from various parts of the country.

Cariliet, Jean-Benard, and Frances Linzee Gordon. *Ethiopia and Eritrea.* **Oakland, CA: Lonely Planet Publications, 2003.**
This volume in the Lonely Planet travel guide series has information on Ethiopia's history, cultures, people, and lots of great ideas for places to visit.

Ethiopia Daily: **News and Current Events**
<http://www.ethiopiadaily.com/>
This on-line publication features news and information on Ethiopian politics, culture, and much more.

Ethiopia: Embassy of Ethiopia. Washington, D.C.
<http://www.ethiopianembassy.org/index.shtml>
The website for Ethiopia's embassy in Washington, D.C., has information on the country's history, people, culture, economy, and government.

Fradin, Dennis Brindell. *Ethiopia.* **New York: Children's Press, 1994.**
This volume in the Enchantment of the World series covers Ethiopia's history, culture, economy, and people.

Gish, Steven. *Ethiopia.* **New York: Marshall Cavendish, 1996.**
This volume in the Cultures of the World series includes a brief history of Ethiopia as well as information on the country's cultures and lifestyles.

Lonely Planet World Guide: **Destination Ethiopia**
<http://www.lonelyplanet.com/destinations/africa/ethiopia/>
The Lonely Planet's World Guide provides an introduction to Ethiopia, as well as up-to-date information for travelers.

Mezlekia, Nega. *Notes from the Hyena's Belly: An Ethiopian Boyhood.* **New York: Picador USA, 2002.**
This memoir, written by a man who grew up during Ethiopia's turbulent 1960s and 1970s, discusses the folktales of his youth, the politics of his times, and his boyhood exploits that tested his mother's patience.

Montgomery, Bertha Vining, and Constance Nabwire. *Cooking the East African Way.* **Minneapolis: Lerner Publications Company, 2002.**
This volume from Lerner's Easy Menu Ethnic Cookbooks series features recipes, as well as cultural and cookery information on several East African countries, including Ethiopia.

Morell, Virginia. *Blue Nile: Ethiopia's River of Magic and Mystery.* **Washington, D.C.: National Geographic Books, 2002.**
Follow a team of *National Geographic* correspondents as they navigate Ethiopia's Blue Nile River via raft, while learning about Ethiopia's history and culture along the way.

Further Reading and Websites

Nomachi, Kazuyoshi. *Bless Ethiopia.* **New York: Odyssey Publications Limited, 1998.**
Filled with stunning photos by an award-winning photographer, this book takes the reader on a colorful journey through Ethiopia's many different cultures and ethnic groups.

Pankhurst, Richard. *The Ethiopians: A History.* **Malden, MA: Blackwell Publishers, 2001.**
This is a history of Ethiopia, written by a scholar who has lived in the country for more than thirty years.

Silverman, Ronald A., ed. *Ethiopia: Traditions of Creativity.* **Seattle: University of Washington Press, 1999.**
Full of vibrant photos and informative essays, this book explores the ancient art of Ethiopia's indigenous peoples.

vgsbooks.com
<http://www.vgsbooks.com>
Visit www.vgsbooks.com, the homepage of the Visual Geography Series®. You can get linked to all sorts of useful on-line information, including geographical, historical, demographic, cultural, and economic websites. The www.vgsbooks.com site is a great resource for late-breaking news and statistics.

Index

Captions for photos appearing on cover and chapter openers:

Cover: A young boy crosses the Little Abbai River, the source of the Blue Nile. The Little Abbai flows into Lake Tana, then becomes the Big Abbai, or Blue Nile River.

pp. 4–5 A young boy sits above the valley of the Blue Nile River.

pp. 8–9 Lake Tana is the largest lake in Ethiopia and is most famous for the sixteenth- and seventeenth-century monasteries scattered among its many islands.

pp. 20–21 The queen of Sheba brings gifts to King Solomon in this nineteenth-century Ethiopian painting titled *The Riches of Solomon.*

pp. 38–39 These young men pose for the camera in Addis Ababa, which has been Ethiopia's capital since 1896.

pp. 46–47 Ruins within the Royal Enclosure of Emperor Fasilides in Gonder. Established in 1636 and known as "Africa's Camelot," Gonder flourished as the nation's capital for about two hundred years.

pp. 56–57 A farmer uses a team of oxen and primitive machinery to plow his field near Weldiya. Lack of modern equipment is an increasing difficulty for subsistence farmers, who rely solely on their crop yields to make a living.

Photo Acknowledgments
The images in this book are used with the permission of: © Nevada Wier, pp. 4–5; © Ron Bell, pp. 6, 11; © Art Directors/TRIP, pp. 8–9, 64; © TRIP/G. Spenceley, p. 10; © 1999, Michele Burgess, pp. 13, 38–39, 41, 46–47; © Word Health Organization/P. Virot, pp. 15, 58, 59; © Gallo Images/CORBIS, pp. 16, 40; © TRIP/J. Sweeney, p. 18; © The Art Archive/Private Collection/Dagli Orti, pp. 20–21; © Victor Englebert, pp. 22, 56–57, 61; © Hulton|Archive by Getty Images, p. 25; © Bettmann/CORBIS, pp. 27, 29; © Scheufler Collection/CORBIS, p. 28; © AP/Wide World Photos, p. 31; © Reuters NewMedia Inc./CORBIS, p. 32; © Jacques M. Chenet/CORBIS, p. 33; © Francoise de Mulder/CORBIS, pp. 34–35; © AFP/Getty Images, pp. 36, 55; © The World Bank Group, p. 42; © Michael S. Lewis/CORBIS, p. 45; © Ricki Rosen/CORBIS, p. 49; © Cory Langley, pp. 51, 68; © TRIP/B. Seed, p. 53; © Dominic Harcourt Webster/ Panos Pictures, pp. 62–63; Laura Westlund, p. 69.

Front Cover: © Nevada Wier, Back Cover: NASA